MURDER IN
PLEASANTON

JOSHUA SUCHON

MURDER IN
PLEASANTON

TINA FAELZ AND
THE SEARCH FOR JUSTICE

THE
History
PRESS

Published by The History Press
Charleston, SC 29403
www.historypress.net

Front cover: Freshman class photo of Tina Faelz. *Courtesy of the Faelz family.*
Back cover, top left: An aerial view, looking south, of the crime scene. *Courtesy of the Alameda County District Attorney's Office.*
Back cover, bottom left: Tina Faelz with her mother, Shirley, and biological father, Ron Penix. *Courtesy of Karin Reiff.*
Back cover, right: Steve Carlson in 2011. *Courtesy of the Bay Area News Group.*

First published 2015

Manufactured in the United States

ISBN 978.1.46711.765.4

Library of Congress Control Number: 2015945062

CONTENTS

Preface   7

1. April 5, 1984   11
2. Who Was Tina Faelz?   27
3. A Kid with Bad ADHD   49
4. The Investigation Begins   59
5. A Community Mourns   77
6. Creepy Gets Creepier   89
7. An Unusual Task Force   103
8. From Pleasanton to Davis   111
9. The DNA Talks   127
10. The Arrest   141
11. The Curious Case of Todd Smith   149
12. Motive?   159
13. The Trial   169
14. Sentencing   183

Bibliography   189
About the Author   191

PREFACE

I always wanted to complete a journalism project that did not involve baseball, mostly as proof to myself that I could do journalism that did not involve home runs and strikeouts. When Steve Carlson was arrested in August 2011 for the murder of Tina Faelz, I thought this was the non-sports assignment I'd been seeking, and I was the ideal to person to tell the story.

I grew up in Pleasanton and lived six blocks down the street from Tina. I was in the fifth grade and a newspaper delivery boy when the murder happened. I went to the same three schools as Tina. My older sister and some of her childhood friends knew Carlson better than most.

The reporting on this book started in September 2011, when I was in San Francisco doing pre- and postgame work for the Los Angeles Dodgers Radio Network. I met Tina's mother, Shirley Orosco, at her home in Pleasanton. She gave her blessing, supported the project and provided valuable contact information, and we talked occasionally over the next few years.

I also met Katie Kelly, Tina's best friend, and started to understand the layers of this tragic story and why it impacted her so much. Over the next four years, I talked to Tina's brother, Drew; her biological father, Ron Penix; stepfather, Steve Faelz; and many other family members. The family shared candid, painful and embarrassing stories. The final book probably doesn't do justice to the full impact Tina's death had on her family and her closest friends. However, without their input, this book either doesn't happen or isn't very compelling.

Approaching people was not easy. How do you explain to a total stranger that you're writing a book about a murder from 1984, and the defendant used to be married to her deceased daughter? That's what it was like introducing myself to Janet Hamilton. She proved to be warm and incredibly helpful, and ultimately, she believed stories like these need to be told. I'm forever grateful to Janet, all her daughter's friends in Davis and to Sarah Whitmire, whose tumultuous relationship with Carlson is heartbreaking. Without their cooperation, I'd have never learned the details about Carlson's time in Davis.

Overwhelmingly, the people I interviewed were friendly and accurately shared what they knew (compared to what "they heard"), and their questions helped me ask better questions. I'm grateful to them all. Well over one hundred people were interviewed, and I probably e-mailed Katie Kelly and Stacy Coleman to ask "one more question" over one hundred times. Their patience and guidance were invaluable.

Some of the people contacted refused to talk or blatantly lied about their association with Carlson, probably out of shame for what they did back in the 1980s. Two people asked for money (and did not accept my counteroffer of a free cup of coffee). Some changed their minds and refused to talk. Some wouldn't talk because it was still too painful. Some felt protective of their neighborhood, which is understandable yet frustrating when you're trying to write a balanced book.

Nineteen months after I started working on this book, I took a new job as the play-by-play announcer for the Albuquerque Isotopes minor league baseball team. For the most part, I'd given up on the book. The trial was delayed so many times, and I was far removed from California. I didn't think I could write the book properly.

Fate is interesting, though. One of my close friends happened to get married in Berkeley the same week that the Carlson trial started in Oakland. I was able to attend the trial. Tina's aunt Karin Reiff and cousin Kim Reiff Buzan encouraged me to finish the book. Karin Reiff spent hours poring through old family photos to share the sweet images you will see.

Still, I needed a publisher. Imagine what The History Press editors must have thought when my proposal came across their desks: a minor league baseball radio announcer in Albuquerque, New Mexico, wants to write a book about a murder in Pleasanton, California, that took place in 1984.

I'd like to thank Will McKay for believing in me, even though my credentials were unique for a true crime. Commissioning editor Megan Laddusaw is a rising star in the publishing industry. If she can coax this book to completion with me, imagine what she'll do editing future books from professional true-crime writers.

When you spend four years working on a project, the final edits are the most nerve-racking. Thanks to production editor Katie Stitely for her patience as I flew around the Pacific Coast League in the summer of 2015 and kept tinkering with the manuscript between broadcasts.

The Pleasanton Police Department and Alameda County District Attorney's Office were generous with their time. Special thanks to Keith Batt, Bill Eastman, James Knox, Stacie Pettigrew, Dana Savage and Gary Tollefson in particular.

Carlson is mostly estranged from his family. He's spent so much time in prison and as a transient that finding people willing to talk for a balanced perspective was nearly impossible. I feel empathy for Carlson's siblings and greatly appreciate elder sister Tanya welcoming me into her home and answering all my questions. I did my best to present his side fairly and accurately.

This book is based on police records, courtroom testimony and the memories of those involved. Because the murder happened over thirty years ago, some inconsistencies will be evident in the sequencing of events by the parties involved. Not every story told to this author was used. This book reflects the most reasonable account of what happened.

It was never my goal to prove Carlson innocent or guilty. That was the jury's responsibility. I wanted to explain life in Pleasanton in 1984, Tina's life, Steve's life before and after the murder, the frustration of the police in solving the case and how this story still resonated with the community three decades later.

1
APRIL 5, 1984

It was the coldest crime scene I've ever seen.
—Bill Eastman

It was Tina Faelz's turn to sit in the front seat of the car on the way to school. Tina was the elder child, a fourteen-year-old freshman at Foothill High. Her younger brother, Drew, an eight-year-old in the fifth grade at Donlon Elementary, was in a bratty mood. Drew wanted to sit in the front seat and jumped in the car first. Upset, Tina fired a few choice words at her younger brother.

"That," Drew said, "was the last conversation I ever had with my sister."

Where to sit in the car was the least of Tina's concerns. Her mother, Shirley, was driving her to school because she had stopped riding the bus. Tina was trying to avoid the neighborhood girls who threatened her, taunted her and made her life miserable at the bus stop, on the bus and on campus.

As they approached the high school, Shirley asked her daughter, "Do you want to change schools?" Tina shook her head. "Not now. I'll wait until the end of this year, then transfer."

Before leaving for school that day, freshman Julie Asplin told her mother that she was staying after school to make up a typing exam. As a result, she'd miss the bus and walk home with her friend Tina Faelz.

"My mom insisted that I didn't stay after school that day," Asplin said. "She had this horrible feeling that something bad was going to happen. She said when I grew up and have my own family, I would understand that feeling."

It was a busy time on campus. Seven more school days remained until spring break. The senior ball was a few weeks after that. Graduation was roughly two months away.

The day was filled with tension on campus. Around 10:00 a.m., wood shop teacher Gary Hicklin heard a loud commotion outside his classroom. Hicklin was told a student was locked in a trash dumpster. Hicklin went outside, unlocked the dumpster and was startled to see a freshman named Steve Carlson inside. Hicklin immediately smelled alcohol on the student's body.

Hicklin observed that Carlson was intoxicated and belligerent. It was an odd interaction; it didn't last long. Hicklin told Carlson to go to the office. Carlson did not. He went in the opposite direction, away from where the classrooms were located on campus, toward the football field and in the direction of where he lived. Hicklin lost sight of Carlson and went back inside his classroom.

"I brought alcohol to school that day, and everybody got drunk, including Steve," sophomore Rob Tremblay said. "He was being stupid to all the girls. All the guys in auto shop, we locked him in there. He was all dirty with food all over him, screaming and yelling…They dropped pot in there or something. We were all silly drunk, and it was easy to coax him into it. Everybody was walking by, kicking it; it echoes in there."

Soon thereafter, freshman Andrew Hartlett said he left campus, along with Todd Smith and Alan "Buck" Rodgers, to check on Carlson. They walked off campus to Carlson's nearby house, knowing his parents were out of town.

"He was drinking vodka," Hartlett said. "I saw him drinking straight from the bottle."

Carlson had the keys to his mother's car. Hartlett said he and Rodgers watched while Smith got in the car. Carlson was sixteen but didn't have a license yet. Carlson went for a brief joyride around the block. Hartlett said he returned to campus with Rodgers and didn't know when Smith came back to school.

Additional tension took place during lunch. A group of three to five girls who had issues with Faelz in the past threw rocks at her. They called her "Tina the Tuna." When school got out, the girls warned Faelz, they were going to kick her ass.

The end of lunch meant the start of fifth period. Two classes remained before school ended. Becky Tantillo was startled to see her friend Faelz enter her classroom because she wasn't in that class.

"Tina was never late for class," said Tantillo, unaware that rocks had been thrown at Faelz minutes prior. "But that day, she made it a point to pay me back the money I loaned her so she could eat, and she was late for her class. That wasn't like her. I asked if she was OK, and she said, 'I'm fine.' But she was being weird that day. I don't know why. She was acting strange. It wasn't like her."

Around 12:30 p.m., assistant principal Jack Keegan had finished eating lunch with other administrators and made his rounds on campus. He was in the northeast corner of the school, near the farm area, when he spotted Carlson. Keegan didn't have any contact with Carlson, other than seeing him walking away from campus, east toward the freeway and where Carlson lived.

Tina Faelz's final class was geography, taught by Barbara

Freshman class photo of Tina Faelz. *Courtesy of the Faelz family.*

Follenfant. Class ended at 2:20 p.m. Before Follenfant went to the girls' locker room to prepare for the softball team's practice, she talked with Faelz for five to ten minutes. The subject wasn't memorable. Follenfant didn't recall that Faelz was upset or scared.

Faelz was supposed to attend detention, which started at 2:30 p.m. and was scheduled to end at 3:15 p.m. Keegan presided over detention and noted that Faelz never showed up. Faelz knew some of the girls who had threatened her earlier in the day were also scheduled for detention. That's possibly why she skipped detention but not definitely why.

What did Faelz do next? She didn't take the bus. She didn't immediately walk home. She wasn't expecting her mother to pick her up. She waited on campus. And waited. She waited at least twenty minutes, perhaps as long as thirty minutes, before she started walking home.

Maybe she was waiting to see if Sirianni and Scarlett had gone to detention and if the coast was clear to walk home without incident. Maybe she was avoiding other girls who bullied her as well. Maybe she was hoping to see the two girls, face her enemies, utilize her recent foray into karate classes and have at them. Maybe she did homework or read a book. Or maybe she was just a lost soul, wandering aimlessly around campus, sitting and reflecting in a quiet place, alone with her thoughts.

Once she finally started walking home, freshman Dean Studemaker was about ten to fifteen feet behind her. They were both walking east, past the baseball field and away from campus. They didn't interact other than Studemaker casually saying, "Bye, Tina," as he turned left and walked north to his house.

Faelz walked by the baseball fields and through the empty football field, ducked through a cutout in the fence that emptied onto Aster Court and turned right onto Muirwood Drive. One street later, she turned left on Lemonwood Way and headed toward the drainage ditch that led to a shortcut that went under Interstate 680 to her neighborhood.

Freshman Sean West was walking home in the same direction. West was no more than five minutes behind Faelz, perhaps two minutes. He knew it was Faelz and where she was going. Their houses were so close, West could see into the backyard of the Faelz house from his bedroom window. Lives were changed by what happened next.

"Tina had just made the turn and gone down [Lemonwood Way]," West said. "My friend Marty drove by and said, 'You want a ride?' I said heck yeah. So I jumped in his Camaro and I took off."

It was about 2:50 p.m., perhaps 2:55 p.m.

Freshmen Weldon Mann and Todd Smith were the next two people to see Faelz alive. Mann knew Faelz well. They both lived on Virgin Islands Court. Mann was a frequent target of little pranks by Faelz and her friend Katie Kelly. They targeted Mann because they both had a crush on him. They would doorbell ditch his house or make a prank phone call. It wasn't malicious. It was two teenage girls trying to get any attention from the popular, cute boy who lived on their street.

"If I remember correctly, we were riding Todd's moped, but I'm not totally sure," Mann said. "We were down there riding around and screwing around. We saw Tina. She was walking toward the culvert. I don't know if somebody was yelling at her or what. I remember spotting her and thinking it was odd. It was a little after school, but not real late. We saw Steve Carlson in his front yard about the same time."

Mann knew Carlson well. They worked together at a restaurant named Augustus washing dishes in the back. One night, they got into a fistfight out by the dumpsters.

"[Carlson] was on his front yard," Mann said. "His parents were out of town. He'd been having during-the-day parties, if I remember right. We spotted him and saw Tina. I looked down at my watch and realized that I was going to be late because my mom was going to pick me up at the top of the school. I was at the bottom of the school. I high-tailed it up to the top of the school. I jumped in the car. I looked at the clock. I was on time. My mom said good job."

It was 3:00 p.m.

LARRY LOVALL WAS A TRUCK DRIVER who spent thirty years driving big rigs up and down the state of California. He'd made stops earlier that day and was now heading south on Interstate 680 to his company's headquarters in San Jose.

Sometime between 3:05 p.m. and 3:15 p.m., Lovall happened to look to his right and noticed something unusual. It looked like a person had fallen in a gully just off the freeway. Nobody else was around the body. Lovall wasn't sure what he saw. It was just a quick glance.

Lovall didn't want to brush it off. He decided to go back for another look. This required him to continue driving south on Interstate 680 to the next exit at Bernal Avenue, make a left at the stop sign where the off-ramp ends and another left to get back onto the freeway heading north for a little over four miles to the 580-680 interchange, circle back around and continue south again.

In Lovall's second trip, he slowed his truck as he approached the location and parked the big rig to the side of what was then a four-lane highway. Lovall got out of the truck, started walking down the steep embankment of the culvert and noticed the body was covered in blood. Lovall didn't go all the way to the body. He saw enough to know she needed immediate help.

Lovall returned to his truck. He drove south on Interstate 680 again, exited at Bernal Avenue, turned left and, this time, drove to the Pleasanton Fairgrounds to find a pay phone.

CURT STONER WAS THE FIRST STUDENT to see the body. Stoner was in the detention period that Faelz skipped. Stoner was ahead of the other students on his way home. When Stoner saw the body, he didn't stick around or look for the closest house to call 911. Instead, he sprinted home as fast as possible. Stoner was so disturbed by what he saw, his older brother called 911 for him.

Sophomores Eric Voellm and Jay Dallimore were the next to see the dead body. The good friends were also walking home after detention. As they approached the entrance to the culvert, they saw a motionless body. They saw papers and books scattered everywhere. And they saw blood—lots and lots of blood. They slowly walked closer to the body, not knowing who it was, their hearts racing with fear and uncertainty. Voellm felt for a pulse. The body was still warm, but he knew the girl was dead.

The boys raced out of the drainage ditch, up the dirt path, across the street and knocked on the front door of 7308 Lemonwood Drive. It was the Carlson house. Nobody answered. The boys then spotted an adult at the house they'd just run past.

It was Michael Toovey, who worked the graveyard shift for the City of San Leandro Public Works and was doing yard work in front of his house. Toovey owned the last house on Ashwood Drive, before it turned into Lemonwood Way. Large trees were along the right side of his house, covering the view of the drainage ditch.

Toovey saw the boys run past his house and across the street. Now, he saw the boys running frantically toward him. They had frightened looks on their faces. They described a girl covered in blood. Toovey asked if she was alive or moving. The boys said no. Toovey called 911 and reported what the boys had told him.

The phone calls by Stoner's older brother and Toovey arrived within seconds of each other at 3:27 p.m., just as the truck driver Lovall was flagging down a uniformed officer at the fairgrounds.

Senior Tony Fisher was in the garage with his friends, a couple blocks down the street on nearby Ashwood Court.

"Some kid I didn't know on a bike was riding down the street, saw us and said, 'Hey you see the dead girl?'" Fisher said. "We thought he was lying. So he took us over. I don't remember if we rode our bikes or walked. We went down there. I walked up toward the body."

It was Fisher, Todd Oelson and Todd Smith who saw the body. Fisher estimated he got about fifteen feet away. "I just remember seeing all her books and papers spread, and just seeing the body laying there. Right when I saw that, that was enough for me…I didn't really want to see the body anymore or get any closer."

Smith did get closer because he didn't think it was a real body. He and his brothers used to cover a go-kart in a way to make it look like a dummy.

"That's what I thought this was," Smith recalled. "All these holes in this sweatshirt cannot be real. No fucking way. That's fake. We started walking away. Somebody said push on the head. That's fake. In that area, there were these sandbags that were dry. They were the shape of concrete bags. They were stacked up the embankment. It felt like I was pushing a concrete bag. I pushed one more time. That's when I threw up in my own mouth. That has never left my mind. I cannot erase that picture, as much as I've tried."

Back at the fairgrounds, Lovall spotted somebody in a police uniform and waved his arms to get their attention. It was Grace Darrell Dickinson, known as G.D. or Gracie Dickinson. It was her fourth year working for the Pleasanton Police Department as a parking control officer, better known as a meter maid.

A bit frantic, Lovall told Dickinson that he had seen a dead body just off the freeway. Dickinson immediately got on the radio and called the dispatcher.

Detective Craig Veteran heard the call from Dickinson on the radio. He was on Division Street, just a few blocks from their location at the fairgrounds. Veteran sped his unmarked car to the fairgrounds and arrived in less than a minute. Lovall explained what he had seen again, this time to Veteran.

Lovall climbed into Veteran's car and described the area accurately. It was easy for Veteran to figure out where to drive. Dickinson drove her marked vehicle behind Veteran's. They didn't take the freeway. They sped west on Bernal Avenue, made a right on Foothill Road and traveled north and then right on Muirwood Drive. The cars turned right on Lemonwood Way and parked at the end of the street.

Veteran was the first officer to arrive at the scene. Neighbor Toovey was still in his front yard. He pointed in the direction of the drainage ditch. Lovall remained in Veteran's car. Veteran and Dickinson searched for the body. At first, they couldn't find it. They didn't know the terrain and paths like the kids did. Veteran went to the freeway to look back, trying to get the same view as the truck driver.

Dickinson could tell from Veteran's body language exactly when he spotted the body. Veteran isn't graceful for his size but was able to climb down the steep embankment to the body. Nobody else was there. Veteran felt for a pulse. It was too late. The girl was dead. Veteran instructed Dickinson to secure the dirt path, making sure no other civilians entered the crime scene.

Gary Tollefson was the working lead detective on crimes against persons when he heard the call over the radio. He was at police headquarters. It was his birthday. He was getting ready to go home a little early. His birthday plans ended immediately. Tollefson arrived at the crime scene at 3:40 p.m., about thirteen minutes after the near-simultaneous 911 calls.

"She was laying there, all cut up," Tollefson said. "Nobody around. She was pretty cut up, but she was pretty pristine. You could tell the kids were traveling through there a lot. Nothing unusual, other than the body…A lot of the cuts were superficial. They weren't real deep."

People v.
Carlson
170014

An officer examines the crime scene on the day of the murder. The body is blurred out by the white flash. *Courtesy of the Alameda County District Attorney's Office.*

Faelz was wearing a black sweater with a purple stripe underneath a purple hoodie and lavender pants. Most of the blood was soaked into her clothes and didn't spill out. Very little blood splattered onto the ground.

Tollefson's initial thought for the murder weapon: "My guess is what we called the folding buck-knife: probably a 4-inch by ¾-inch blade. It looked like it was pretty sharp."

Police Chief Bill Eastman was in a meeting when the 911 calls were made. He arrived a few minutes after Tollefson. One everlasting image remains of what he saw. "It was the coldest crime scene that I've ever seen," Eastman said. "I've seen dozens of homicides. There was nothing there."

Nothing meant no clues.

Sergeant Michael Stewart brought a camera kit to the crime scene for Tollefson. As lead detective, Tollefson was in charge of gathering evidence and taking pictures. Tollefson took pictures of the crime scene with his thirty-five-milimeter Canon. He used two rolls of film, for a total of forty-eight pictures.

Stewart looked for the murder weapon or any clues. He walked underneath Interstate 680 through the tunnel, reaching the other side. Nothing significant

People v.
Carlson
170014

Detective Don Saulsbury used a metal detector in the high grass field to look for a murder weapon or any clues on the day of the murder. *Courtesy of the Alameda County District Attorney's Office.*

was found. Stewart interviewed Voellm and Dallimore together, then truck driver Lovall and then the trio of Fisher, Oelson and Smith.

Above the body, in a tree that was covered in shrubbery, Tollefson spotted a purse. The tree was eight to ten feet in height. Tollefson was not wearing plastic gloves. Tollefson would later testify that he did not remember how he got the purse out of the tree. He did not notice any blood on the purse. He was mindful of not getting his fingerprints on the purse. Tollefson recalled holding the purse by the evidence tag he placed on the zipper. He placed the purse inside a brown grocery bag.

Detective Don Saulsbury's first job was to search for fingerprints. In an area that was mostly dirt and trees, none were available on the chain-link fence or the metal break that students climbed through to reach the tunnel. When a metal detector was borrowed from the water department, Saulsbury searched the chest-high grass area for a murder weapon. He found nothing.

It was easy for police to identify the victim. Tina Faelz's name was written on two books and papers inside a blue binder, which were scattered around her body.

At 3:40 p.m., detective Robert Fracoli arrived on the scene. Fracoli was provided the name Tina Faelz by Lieutenant Dave Freeman and instructed to find out information about her at the school. Fracoli left at 3:43 p.m. He entered the high school's administration building a few minutes later, was greeted by assistant principals Edith Stock and Jack Keegan and told them there had been a stabbing and he needed the records of Tina Faelz.

Stock provided an attendance card and a picture of Faelz. Fracoli returned to the crime scene with the identification. Fracoli went back to the high school for a second time to obtain more information. He learned that Barbara Follenfant was the teacher for Faelz's last class of the day. Follenfant told the detective she thought she saw Faelz leaving the school in an orange and white Volkswagen bus. Fracoli then returned to the police station and picked up a clergy member to assist with notifying the mother.

It was a busy day for Foothill High athletic teams and after-school programs. The track team was off campus in a tri-meet with Monte Vista High and the hosts at Dublin High. The tennis team was hosting Livermore High that day, but there were no tennis courts on Foothill's campus back then. The matches took place at Muirwood Community Park, one mile north of the crime scene, off Muirwood Drive. The golf team hosted crosstown rivals Amador Valley High at Castlewood Country Club, about four and a half miles south, off Foothill Road. The varsity softball team was practicing on campus. Their field was located at the back of campus just off Muirwood Drive, less than half a mile from the crime scene.

"I remember it was an absolutely gorgeous day," said Joy Erven, a freshman catcher on the varsity softball team. "It was sunny, clear skies. It's something I remembered very vividly because we were standing on the field and heard the [police] sirens. They were so loud, we all stopped. I wondered, 'What happened?' We all stopped and looked in that direction. And then, it was like a pause. We kept playing."

Matt Sweeney, before becoming the school's most successful varsity football coach, was an assistant coach for the junior varsity baseball team. Sweeney distinctly recalled seeing and hearing police cars coming into the nearby neighborhood. Practice was almost over anyway, and they didn't stop. It wasn't until practice ended that they learned a student had been murdered.

The marching band was in Orlando, Florida, that week for a prestigious competition and would take sixth place nationally.

The number of athletic teams playing games off campus, and the band being out of town, was significant. It meant fewer students were taking the shortcut home that day. Fewer students were hanging out around campus to watch the games. The band wasn't practicing on the nearby football field. No other adults or coaches or umpires were on campus for a sporting event. The campus was unusually quiet.

That also meant fewer people were around to witness the killing or prevent it from ever happening. It proved to be the ideal day for a murder to take place so close to a busy high school. But given all those bodies going in so many directions—and given the unpredictability of students on any given day, especially when sports are involved—you would be foolish to plan a murder in that spot, in that time and on that day and feel like nobody would see it.

It was a complete fluke that nobody saw the murder.

AMY CARLSON AND HER FRIEND LISA BENHAM stayed after school at Wells Middle School in Dublin. Amy had a theater rehearsal. Lisa stayed to get help in computers. Benham recalled that Tanya Carlson, the elder sister of Amy, was supposed to pick them up from school. When she didn't show up, the seventh-grade girls called from a pay phone.

Tanya told the girls a murder had taken place across from the house, and she couldn't pick them up. Another parent ended up giving the girls a ride. They arrived home sometime after 4:00 p.m. By that time, police cars were all over the streets. Some neighborhood mothers told their children to stay inside so they wouldn't be accused of something incorrectly.

On the other side of Interstate 680, in the Valley Trails neighborhood, eight-year-old Drew Faelz was riding his bike on the court of the family's Virgin Islands home. It was about 4:45 p.m.

His sister wasn't home from school yet. That was unusual but not totally unheard of. The previous day, Tina hadn't gotten home until about the same time. She told her mother that she was at the Stoneridge Mall, which was uncommon. Faelz was not into shopping. Usually, Faelz came straight home from school and watched soap operas.

Recently divorced single mother Shirley Faelz cleaned houses on the side for extra money. She had cleaned two or three that day. Shirley told Drew she was going to the bank at Valley and Hopyard. She'd return in fifteen to twenty minutes.

Drew Faelz rode his bicycle to this park when he saw a police car come down his street on the day of the murder. His old house is in the middle of the photo, where the basketball hoop is located. *Photo by the author.*

"Right after she left, I saw the [unmarked] car come down the street," Drew said. "From watching TV shows, I knew something was wrong. My sister wasn't home. I rode up to the park and got away from them. Right then, I saw that car park in front of my house. They knocked on the door when I was in the park."

Shirley Faelz was still at the bank. Nobody answered the door.

"I came back, they saw me and asked if I lived there," continued Drew. "I said, 'Yeah.' They asked, 'Do you have any good friends in the neighborhood?' The Haywards were across the street. They took me over there. I stayed there until later that evening."

When Shirley Faelz arrived back home from the bank, at approximately 5:00 p.m., she was greeted by Detective Fracoli and a priest. "My daughter is dead," was her immediate thought. Fracoli stayed at the Faelz house, asked questions and tried to learn information on who might be responsible.

Shirley asked her brother-in-law Don Reiff to identify the body at the morgue.

"They removed the cover on her," Reiff recalled. "It was just a brutal, brutal sight. Something that never leaves your mind, or your memory, to see a young girl laying there with wounds on her arms and hands and face and body. Just ridiculous. It was so massive. You couldn't believe it happened."

The family gathered at Shirley's house and stayed the rest of the night.

"Shirley was just in a total daze," said Karin Reiff, the younger sister of Shirley by eighteen months. "She showed no emotion at all. She had a boyfriend that nobody liked, Keith Fitzwater. He organized everybody coming over and protecting Shirley. He was pretty good that night, in terms of taking care of Shirley and keeping people corralled. Shirley just wandered. Didn't really talk about it at all."

AT 4:30 P.M., GRACIE DICKINSON DROVE the truck driver back to his car at the fairgrounds and the students who found the body to their homes in the Valley Trails neighborhood. They also lived a few courts over from the Faelz residence.

Jeff Wainwright was in the park that divided the neighborhood in half. He saw his friends Eric Voellm and Jay Dallimore in the back of a police car and assumed they were in trouble. Wainwright and a couple friends raced to the police car to find out what had happened. The boys shared the news of their grisly discovery.

"It just blew up from there," Wainwright said. "I couldn't get home quick enough to tell my parents. Next thing you knew, people down the street knew."

Freshman Jimmy Poppell, who turned fifteen years old that day, spent the afternoon riding his Redline MXIII dirt bike around the neighborhood. He was at the park with other kids as Voellm and Dallimore continued to share what they had discovered.

"I remember Jay's face was ghost white," Poppell wrote on his personal blog in 2012. "He was visibly shaken. When he spoke, his voice was trembling as he told us the gory details and what he saw. The emotions going through my body were fear, disbelief, anger and an overwhelming sadness."

When softball practice ended, Erven received a ride to her home in the Valley Trails neighborhood. Erven lived three blocks from the Faelz home. She wasn't a close friend of Faelz, but lockers were arranged alphabetically at school, and many teachers sat their students in desks by last name. As a result, Erven and Faelz were physically next to each other a lot.

"They were talking to my brother in the front yard, and it was like, 'Oh my God! Oh my God!'" Erven said. "That's how we heard what happened. At that age, I truly believed that we were going to have a nuclear war at any moment. That movie had just come out, *The Day After*. We'd have earthquakes drills and hide under the kitchen table. We really thought the sky was falling. Then to have somebody killed that you know, that you took the bus with, that you sat behind, who had a locker right above yours? It was absolutely terrifying."

Word spread everywhere. Kids raced to the phone to tell friends. They told anybody who walked by their houses. It was pandemonium in the Valley Trails neighborhood.

One neighborhood over in Val Vista, Stacy Coleman was with a group of friends, including Kristen Hendershott and Kim Scola. Coleman doesn't remember the exact details of how they learned the news. There were no text messages, no Facebook and no cell phones. Information trickled in through a string of phone calls on landlines and kids riding bicycles through the street like messengers. Still, the way Tina Faelz's closest friends learned about the murder was like a newswire.

"We heard somebody was killed," Coleman said. "Then we heard it was somebody from Foothill. Then we heard where they were killed, and we were saying, 'Wow that's really weird somebody from our school got killed. We might know somebody who got killed.' Then we started thinking about, well, where she got killed. Who do we know that walks home that way? We knew it was somebody from Valley Trails or Val Vista because that's who walked that way. We started thinking and calling people."

Coleman called Tina Faelz to make sure her friend was safe.

"We asked to talk to Tina," Coleman said. "It was a man who answered the phone. We knew it wasn't her mom's boyfriend. It wasn't his voice. We asked for Tina. They said, 'You can't talk to Tina right now, she's not here,' or something like that. We asked to talk with Shirley and they said, 'It's not a good time' and hung up."

Not satisfied with the response, one of the girls' mothers called back to the Faelz house. They confirmed that Tina was the victim.

Another one of those phone calls came to Julie Asplin. Her first thought was that she was supposed to walk home from school with Faelz that day. After her mother's bizarre plea in the morning to come straight home, Asplin wasn't initially sure if she would take her mother's advice or not.

Ultimately, she left school on time. Asplin's grief was compounded by the uncertainty of what was changed by her decision to come straight home.

"That could have been me," Asplin said. "That could have been both of us. Maybe it wouldn't have happened, if I did walk home with her. A lot of 'what ifs.' I don't recall what time we found out she was killed. I think it was late that night. I remember crying all night long. It was just a weird feeling that came over me. Somebody that I knew, something terrible happened in a community that was supposed to be safe."

Sunset was at 6:34 p.m. As the sky went from light to dark, the work continued for the entire Pleasanton Police Department, gathering and collecting evidence, filing the evidence and beginning an investigation. It was an emotional night. At that time, Pleasanton was a town of just forty-two thousand people. There had been only five murders in Pleasanton since World War II. None of the previous victims was a child.

Bill Eastman, the Pleasanton police chief, had two daughters who attended Foothill High. Lead Detective Gary Tollefson also had a teenage daughter at Foothill. They didn't need to say it aloud. It could have been their daughters. This was personal.

Eastman told reporters that Faelz was stabbed repeatedly with a knife in her back, side and face. But he held back the actual number of stab wounds. He didn't want the community more astonished than they already were.

"This is a horrid crime," Eastman told the media. "All available resources are being committed to solve it."

Eastman emphasized to reporters that Faelz was not sexually assaulted and not robbed. He added there was no doubt she was killed in that exact spot. The *Valley Times* reported that police were searching for a hitchhiker and a student carrying a square blue backpack.

The chief speculated the girl might have been killed as revenge. He said there's nothing to suspect the killing was drug related. Similarly, Eastman said police had no evidence to suggest one of her peers might be responsible but believed the girl might have known her attacker.

Tina Faelz had only been on campus for seven months and was pretty anonymous except for a handful of close friends and the girls who made her life miserable.

"I couldn't have picked her out of a crowd of two," admitted Assistant Principal Keegan. "If they said, 'Here's a group of girls, pick out Tina Faelz.' I couldn't do it."

One of the first things that Eastman's department and Foothill High's administration needed to figure out: just who was Tina Faelz?

2
WHO WAS TINA FAELZ?

She could make me laugh until I nearly peed my pants.
—Stacy Coleman

APRIL 27, 1969–APRIL 4, 1984

Ron Penix was among the thousands of youths drawn to San Francisco for the counterculture lifestyle in the late 1960s. Penix and some of his hippy friends moved from the state of Washington to San Francisco. He was working at a dive on Market Street called the Donut Palace when he met a woman named Shirley Griffith. She was the eldest of five children, not too many years removed from Canyon High in Castro Valley, a suburb twenty-six miles southeast of San Francisco.

"We instantly bonded," Penix said. "We lived for a few months on spare change. I finally called home and got enough money to go home. I was a telephone lineman at the time. I went back into that work, doing power-line work and traveling all over."

Ron Penix and Shirley Griffith were married in 1968 at a restaurant where Ron's mother worked as a bartender. Most of Shirley's family had never met him. The couple had a child the next year. Tina Marie Penix was born on April 27, 1969.

"She was a beautiful little blond girl," Penix said. "Healthy. Red cheeks. Absolutely adorable. I remember her laughing and being carefree. Of

Shirley Faelz in 1971 with her daughter, Tina, and their dog. *Courtesy of Karin Reiff.*

course, being the person that I was at the time, I went out and got drunk to celebrate…I was not a good father. I was an alcoholic and—just not a good husband. Unfortunately, Tina and Shirley paid a price for that."

About a year later, Shirley had had enough. She packed a suitcase and took a bus back to California, along with her daughter, Tina. Penix drove down to San Francisco to see his wife and daughter a few months later.

"Of course, I was drunk," Penix said. "Being the male pig that I was, I told her, 'You can get home the same way you got here—on a bus.' The rest is history."

Shirley came up to retrieve the rest of their belongings. Penix made virtually no attempt to maintain custody of his daughter Tina. He showed scant interest in coming to California to visit.

Back in her hometown of Castro Valley, Shirley Griffith ran into an old crush from high school. His name was Steve Faelz. Crush is actually an understatement. Object of infatuation might be more accurate.

As a kid, Faelz played sports at Norbridge Elementary with his friends. Shirley would show up, watch them play and mostly stare at Steve. Faelz picked up a job at Common Auto Supply his junior year in high school. Shirley's father would come into the store to look around, while Shirley looked through the window. Faelz knew that several auto supply stores were located closer to the Griffiths' house. He was flattered but didn't pay much attention to the girl.

"I wasn't sophisticated or suave," Faelz said. "I wasn't a ladies man. I was grunt and bluff."

After high school, Steve Faelz went to the Marine Corps and returned just shy of his twenty-first birthday. He lived with his parents for a few months, saving up money by working at Caterpillar Tractor in Castro Valley. One day, Shirley Griffith called Faelz out of the blue and asked if he wanted to get together with her. They went to the San Francisco Zoo on their date—along with Shirley's little girl, Tina—and had a nice time.

"We got together and dated a few more times," Faelz said. "The next thing you know, she asked if we wanted to get an apartment and live together. I said, 'OK, let's try that.' It was a real impetuous, youthful decision."

They rented an apartment in San Leandro on 165th Avenue. A few months later, Faelz was hired by the Castro Valley Fire Department and began his training. Around the fall of 1971, Shirley met with a lawyer in downtown Hayward, not far from the fire station, to finalize the divorce from Ron Penix.

Shirley and Tina were walking on a sidewalk near Castro Valley Boulevard and Redwood Road when they tried hurrying across the street to catch a bus. An oncoming car didn't see them in time to brake and slammed into them. Shirley's injuries were relatively minor. Tina was severely hurt.

"She ended up being in Stanford Children Hospital for a couple months," Faelz said. "She was in a full body cast. It went around her head and shoulders and down to her waist. She had surgery to the back of her foot. We'd go there every chance we got to see her through that ordeal. We made numerous trips. She wasn't on life support. But it was a major recovery because she was in a body cast for quite awhile."

Shirley carried Tina everywhere in a big body cast. Tina survived, made a full recovery and returned home. Steve and Shirley moved into a place on Queens Street in Castro Valley around 1972, a nice house with a backyard

Tina Faelz and her mother, Shirley, at Christmastime in 1973. *Courtesy of Karin Reiff.*

and garden. It was Steve's first experience around a young child, but it was something he enjoyed.

Steve Faelz and Shirley Griffiths were married in 1973. Tina was four years old. Steve was a full-time employee of the fire department in Castro Valley, just like his father. They bought a house on Lobert Street and lived there for a couple years.

Steve adopted Tina, and she took his last name. Ron Penix agreed that it was in Tina's best interest.

On November 27, 1975, Shirley and Steve welcomed a child into the world. Drew Allan Faelz was six years younger than his sister, but the two shared a bond that defied their age gap.

Tina holds her little brother in 1976. *Courtesy of Karin Reiff.*

The Valley Trails neighborhood of Pleasanton was created in 1968 and mostly finished by 1971, although small changes continued for the next two decades. It was builder Morrison Homes' foray into the new lifestyle communities gaining popularity in town.

In one advertisement, Valley Trails is described as "a unique, totally different cul-de-sac land plan. A new contained community features a wide, landscaped park running through the community to the elementary school site. In this pastoral green belt, your children will have room to roam, to run, to ramble with complete safety."

All the houses were initially one of five models. The lots ranged from 1,300 to 1,900 square feet. A newspaper advertisement in 1972 offered homes priced at $34,040.

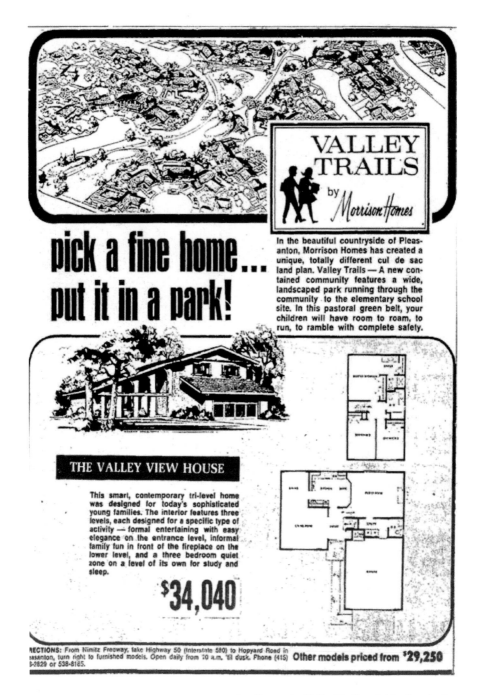

This advertisement helped lure many young families to the Valley Trails neighborhood of Pleasanton in the 1970s. *From the author's personal collection.*

Tina Faelz and her family moved into the Valley Trails neighborhood in the mid-1970s. *Photo by the author.*

The streets in Valley Trails were named after national parks. From the south entrance off Hopyard Road, the streets were named Harpers Ferry Court, Isle Royal Court, Cumberland Gap Court, Zion Canyon Court, Kings Canyon Court, Yellowstone Court, Wind Cave Court and Virgin Islands Court. In those days, Pleasanton was the opposite of the affluent upper-middle-class suburb it has become.

"It was the boonies," said Eddie Gallagher, whose family was the fourth to move into Valley Trails in 1968. He moved back to his old neighborhood in his late thirties. "It's funny now. You have all these rich people in Pleasanton. We lived in Pleasanton because we were poor. It was more expensive to live over the hill in San Leandro or Castro Valley. There was nothing out here."

In 1976, Shirley, Steve, Tina and Drew Faelz moved into a house near the end of Virgin Islands Court.

"Life was good," Steve said. "It's a nice community. We had good neighbors. No problems with anybody. The kids were adjusted well. Tina played soccer. Drew played soccer. I had a few fireman friends who lived in Valley Trails and a couple in the other neighborhood over, in Val Vista. We liked going to downtown Pleasanton. It was an old, rustic downtown. We liked going down there for dinner and pizza a lot."

Tina Faelz is on the second row, far left, giving the OK sign with her fingers. *Courtesy of Jackie Carleton Picton.*

Katie Kelly was ecstatic. A new family had moved onto her court, with a girl the same age. She would have a new friend. However, the first time Tina and Drew came over to play, it was a disaster. The Faelz kids were a terror, breaking practically all of Katie's toys.

This book's author, just before turning eight years old, moved into the Valley Trails neighborhood with his family in the summer of 1981—six courts down the street from the Faelz residence.

The 6.1-acre greenbelt that ran through the heart of the neighborhood was always filled with kids. They'd ride bikes, play soccer, baseball or football or just hang out. Sometimes, kids met for fistfights to settle their differences. Overall, it was safe. You could walk in the dark without fear. The worst thing that would happen is stumbling on older teenagers drinking booze, smoking a little pot or making out.

Tina played soccer for three to four seasons. Her parents attended almost every game. In one game, Tina got a bloody nose, and her fireman father provided first aid on the field.

1984 ··· 1985

THOMAS H DONLON SCHOOL

Donlon Elementary in 1984. The author was in the fifth grade and Drew Faelz was in the second grade at the time of the murder. *From the Donlon Elementary School 1985 yearbook, courtesy of the author's collection.*

Children in Valley Trails attended Donlon Elementary, centered in the middle of the nearby Val Vista neighborhood. It was 1.3 miles to drive from the Faelz home to the school. If you walked or rode a bike, which most students did, it was a little shorter when you cut through the 7-11 parking lot at the corner of Hopyard Road and West Las Positas Boulevard.

Shirley Faelz worked at that 7-11, which made her recognizable to kids in the neighborhood. That 7-11 had video games in the front left corner. If a student was late for school, it was probably because he was attempting to get the highest score on Donkey Kong.

"Every kid in Valley Trails or Val Vista knew her [Tina's] mom," Gallagher said. "We nicknamed her E.T. because she was short and she kinda looked similar like E.T. One kid said it, and it stuck."

Living in Valley Trails in the 1970s and early 1980s was just like the cheerful advertisement. All you needed was a bicycle, and the city was yours to explore. Pleasanton didn't have a movie theater in those days, but kids like Tina Faelz and her friend Lorraine Vener thought nothing about making the four-mile bike ride to the two movie theaters across the freeway in Dublin.

Tina Faelz is in the second row, far right. *Courtesy of Jackie Carleton Picton.*

"It was so simple," Vener said. "In the summertime, we would play football until midnight. Our parents didn't need to be out front or anything. Nobody ever worried about anything. We all knew everybody. Parents were close. Kids were close. Life was really simple. We didn't have cell phones and pagers. Our parents didn't worry if we came home late because they knew our friends."

The parents on Virgin Islands Court were close. Pam and Don Carleton (not to be confused with the Carlsons) had a daughter named Jackie. They threw parties for the young kids at their house and delighted in taking photos.

"Tina was always a sweet girl," said Don Carleton, whose daughter Jackie was a year younger than Tina. "Always smiling and sweet. Acted a little shy…I couldn't imagine her hanging around a bunch of rough people, a rough crowd."

Those who didn't know Faelz described her as shy and reserved. Her closest friends, those she trusted, knew her as the opposite.

At a birthday party, Tina Faelz is on the back row, second from the left. *Courtesy of Jackie Carleton Picton.*

"She could make me laugh until I nearly peed my pants," said Stacy Coleman, a friend of Tina's since elementary school. "She was hysterically funny. She was a big joker. She could make anything into a joke. I played softball with her. I played on the playground at Donlon School with her. I was in Girl Scouts and Brownies with her. She could make faces like you wouldn't believe."

Another favorite activity for Faelz was climbing trees, which led to a cherished memory of Vener.

"A couple times we went to the movies, and there was a gas station right around the corner from it," Vener said. "There was a tree back there. We were up there one time and...oh my God, she had chew, or Skoal! She'd picked it up from somewhere or somebody gave it to her. It made me very dizzy, and I fell out of the tree. We were both laughing so hard. Then I remember her getting serious. Then I told her I was fine, and so we started laughing again."

STEVE AND SHIRLEY FAELZ'S RELATIONSHIP ended around 1982. Shirley suspected that her husband was having an affair—and not just any affair. Shirley thought it was with her younger brother's wife. Shirley told the family of her suspicions. They thought she was crazy. As it turned out, Shirley was correct. Steve Faelz moved out of the house on Virgin Islands Court in Pleasanton and back to Castro Valley with a woman who used to be his sister-in-law.

"That made the family complicated," said Kim Reiff Buzan, a younger cousin of Tina. "The family was kinda messed up. Drew's cousins became his brothers. His aunt became his stepmom. There were a lot of family functions that became really weird. It was not a normal thing."

Shirley remained in Pleasanton as a single mother to raise Tina and Drew on a meager salary from working at a 7-11, any houses she could clean, the child support Steve provided and turning rooms into bedrooms that could be rented to strangers.

"My mom wasn't handling the divorce too well," Drew said. "My sister helped raised me. She babysat me a lot. I remember she was a very good role model. At the same time, she was goofy and fun, like a sister."

The parents fought over custody of the children. Steve wanted a fifty/fifty split. He was denied. The custodial order called for Steve to get both children every other weekend, plus two weeks in the summer.

Lisa Celestre and Tina Faelz became close friends through their mothers. Both moms worked at 7-11; both were divorced; both went to bars at night,

Tina was the eldest of all her cousins. This is her with her cousin Kim. *Courtesy of Karin Reiff.*

usually ending up at the Popi Lounge at Hopyard Road and Valley Drive. The teenage girls spent a lot of time together at night while their moms were out drinking.

"I loved Tina's personality," Celestre said. "I'd babysit Drew every once in awhile. She came over to our house because we had a pool. She had this dictionary, and the way she hid her money was in the pages of the dictionary. It was so funny. I loved it. It was such a neat idea."

The owner of the Popi Lounge arranged group outings for employees and regulars. They'd have weekend barbecues or trips to Del Valle Regional Park. That's when Tina became friends with Lisa Hall.

"We always had fun," Hall said. "Tina was a lot like me. I was kinda like that nerdy outcast person. I know that's not the right terminology. We just connected. It didn't matter who you were. There was none of the other kids who made fun of you, none of the harassing. We went into the lake, we went on hikes, that kind of stuff. I just remember us always laughing and having fun. To me, she was fun to be around. But then, when we got around to going back to school, or when we got around the outside of that element, she was very quiet and didn't talk a lot."

The first time Tina Faelz and Katie Kelly played together, it ended in broken toys and disaster. In the years that followed, they played in fabled kickball games on their cul-de-sac. Tina was known for her vague application of kickball rules, a combination of charming and maddening for participants. Since most of the kids were younger, Tina's on-the-fly rules were accepted, despite the protests of Kelly.

The turning point in their friendship came in the sixth grade, during Mrs. Killoran's poetry assignment. Kelly wrote a long poem about saving and respecting animals and delivered it emotionally. The teacher was stunned that so many lines rhymed, wiped away her own tears and effusively praised Kelly to the class.

Kelly walked home, feeling good, along with classmate Becky Vassis. Then she heard a voice from behind her.

"Save the polar bears! Because without polar bears, we will have no air!"

It was Tina Faelz, her neighbor. Kelly's hair stood on end. That wasn't the point of the poem. Kelly wanted to be upset at Tina for mocking her, but she couldn't bring herself to be mad. Something about Tina's voice made it funny, not mean. All Kelly could do was laugh.

For the next three years, Tina and Katie Kelly were inseparable. In the summer, they swam for hours at the Pleasanton Aquatic Center until their eyes turned red. They rode bikes across town to hidden creeks or Bob's Big Boy. They talked about things that scared them, about what color people dreamed in before color movies, what lies in the universe beyond the stars—and, of course, what boys they liked.

The other staple of Tina and Katie's friendship was doorbell ditching and prank calling. Nobody was immune from the duo's pranks. They'd do it to the boys they had crushes on, the girls they disliked and total strangers. Tina was the ringleader, but Katie was stride-for-stride with her. Once, after a doorbell-ditch mission, they sat in Kelly's father's car, a Ford Pinto, for a stakeout.

"You know, Katie," Tina said, "we make a pretty good team."

Katie's mom said they laughed too much. They laughed about silly things, at the worst possible times, which made people around them angry—which made it even more funny to the girls. They'd laugh so hard that they'd literally pee their pants.

Embarrassed, they would tie sweatshirts or other clothing items around their waists to hide the wet spots. Other girls would mock their style, tell them they looked dumb and ask if that was a fashion statement. Rather than admitting the truth, the friends would say it was their own fashion statement.

In the early 1980s, all the phone numbers in Pleasanton began with 846 or 462. Katie would punch in random phone numbers and then Tina would grab the phone and do her magic with calls that would make Bart Simpson proud.

"Well, hello there! Is your refrigerator running?"

"Well, you better go catch it, before it gets out the door."

Katie's parents would have friends over to the house, and they'd gather in the backyard. Tina would go upstairs to the bedroom of Katie's sister, which didn't have a screen, and delicately pour water onto the heads of unsuspecting visitors.

All these pranks were hysterical for Tina's closest friends but not necessarily for everybody else, especially the popular girls in the neighborhood.

"Tina wasn't always very nice," admitted her friend Stacy Coleman. "She played a lot of practical jokes on people. That's why she was funny. Sometimes, it was at somebody else's expense, and they didn't think it was funny. There were a lot of people who seriously didn't like her."

Faelz's relationship with the four Sirianni children, who lived on the same street, changed over the years. Tina was once friends with Kathy, but they grew apart and later became verbally combative. Dave Sirianni tried to help Tina after she fell off her bicycle one day, and Tina screamed loudly until her mother came outside to see what was going on.

One day, Tina and Katie played a prank on Steve Sirianni, the youngest of the four Sirianni children. Steve fell off his bike but didn't suffer a serious injury. That drew the ire of Steve's older sister, Kathy Sirianni, and contributed to tension that lasted years.

One unforgettable day, Tina and Katie were walking home from the bus stop. Two girls waited in the bushes and then jumped out at them, threatening violence.

"Would you like us to kick your asses today?" they asked. "Or do you want us to get the gang?"

It wasn't a real gang. This wasn't *Girlz n the Hood* or South Central Los Angeles. It was still Pleasanton. This was just a larger group of girls, and gang was used for lack of a better word. Kelly requested the gang. Of course, that was taken the wrong way, drawing the girls' ire even more for Kelly being a smartass. Through gentle negotiations, the friends made it home unscathed.

Tina's pranks and rebellion were based, to some degree, on problems at home. Tina's mother, Shirley, did not handle the divorce well. She turned a family room into another bedroom so she could rent it out to make money. People were coming and going in the house regularly.

Shirley dated a man named Keith Fitzwater for a few years. He moved into the house with Shirley and her two kids. Fitzwater was a drug user. Family members saw bruises on Shirley's body and suspected that he physically abused her. Shirley always denied it.

The relationship between Tina and Fitzwater was troublesome. Fitzwater spent enough time alone with Tina in her room that friends and family felt was inappropriate. According to friends, Tina told her mother about one unwanted advance, when Tina awoke in her bed to find Fitzwater's hand under the blanket on her leg. Shirley didn't believe her daughter and refused to kick Fitzwater out of the house.

Tina told her friends that she didn't want her mom to marry Fitzwater. Yet Tina occasionally told friends she was in love with him, too. Her friends didn't know what to think. Even at age fourteen, Tina's closest friends realized her erratic behavior and razor tongue were byproducts of an unstable home life.

Even if the scars weren't visible, the signs were evident to one of Shirley's closest friends.

"Tina always wanted attention because she didn't have too many friends at the school because of the way she acted," said Diane Jones, who got the job at 7-11 with the help of her friend Shirley. "She always craved for attention from people at home. I thought one day, 'Something is going to happen to this girl.'"

IN THE FALL OF 1983, Tina began her freshman year at Foothill High. Drugs and alcohol were widespread on campus, and not just for the seniors and juniors either. Many students began experimenting in junior high. Girls brazenly shoulder-tapped older guys outside liquor stores and easily obtained the booze. Some liquor store owners wouldn't bother checking an ID, especially if the girl was cute and flirty.

At school dances, more students were drunk than sober. The most belligerent would get caught. The more subtly intoxicated would avoid trouble. It wasn't just special occasions, like a dance, that prompted the students to party. On average, assistant principal Jack Keegan would suspend one to two students every week for being drunk during school hours. One memorable day at lunch, Keegan approached a male student holding a big Slurpee cup. He opened it, took a smell and realized the entire cup was filled with vodka.

"When you look at the parenting of the '80s, it was a more *relaxed* environment, shall we say," said Pat Keegan, the wife of the assistant principal and herself a special education teacher at the high school. "Even to have smoking allowed on campus, I thought that was horrible."

It wasn't legal for teenagers to buy cigarettes in a store in 1984. But somehow, for reasons hard to explain, there was a designated smoking section on Foothill High's campus for students.

"Yes, we had a smoking section," said Jack Keegan, shaking his head in disbelief. "We had problems with parents having parties where they would allow the beer and booze and everything else. As Pat says, it was pretty liberal in some of those areas. You kind of looked at it, like, 'We're trying to bring the students along, and we have to bring the parents along, too?' Their feeling was, they could keep them home, so they could control it there."

The divorce rate was skyrocketing. Many kids divided their time between two houses, doubling their opportunities to raid liquor cabinets. In the competition for child custody and child support, some parents realized that leniency toward alcohol consumption was a means to curry favorite status from their children.

Tina Faelz wasn't a drinker and wasn't into drugs. She wasn't an athlete and wasn't a cheerleader. She didn't take drama or leadership classes or write for the school paper or play in the band or participate in any other after-school programs. She struggled to fit in. She was quiet and shy to most, yet a fondness for pranks and a perceived smart mouth made her despised by others.

Rocks were thrown at Faelz and Kelly as they waited at the bus stop. Other girls would ask, "Can you stand somewhere else so we don't accidentally get hit by a rock?" Faelz and Kelly tried going to a different bus stop, which would get them on the bus sooner, but it didn't help.

"They would tease her," remembered April Roach, another freshman who lived across the greenbelt in Valley Trails. "They called her gay. They called her ugly. I would say, 'Tina, come sit with me.' She'd sit on the inside, next to the window. I guess I was playing mother hen for her. She had a cute laugh. When you heard her giggle, it made you giggle. She had a sweet personality. She was small in stature, and she was so sweet. Unfortunately, she did get picked on."

In retrospect, Kelly always thought they were outcasts because of how much fun they were having outside, at an age when girls were supposed to be doing their hair and talking about fashion all day. When their peers were obsessing over makeup, Faelz and Kelly were riding Big Wheels and performing bike stunts.

In 1984, kids tore a hole in the fence to reach the Creek in the Valley Trails neighborhood. Nowadays, there's an opening for joggers and bicycle riders to access the area. *Photo by the author.*

Tina was fearless when it came to riding her bicycle. Sometime early in 1984, she showed up unannounced at Steve Faelz's house in Castro Valley to discuss something in person. Tina had traversed over fifteen miles, including a steep incline over the hills separating the cities, on her bike.

By the spring semester of 1984, the bullying caused Faelz to stop taking the bus entirely. Sometimes, Shirley picked up her daughter from school. Oddly, Tina wasn't interested in riding her bike to school.

Most of the time, Tina walked home, taking a shortcut underneath the freeway. It was an area known by kids as the "Creek."

As the population of Pleasanton increased in the early 1970s, Amador Valley High was no longer big enough to accommodate all the students. The city's second high school was added in 1973, aptly named Foothill High, located on Foothill Road and literally at the foot of the hill. The school's first year was freshman only. Each year, a new freshman class was added, and the first graduating class was in 1977.

This is the opening on the Valley Trails (east side) of Interstate 680. Kids would enter here on the way to Foothill High and exit here on the way home from school. *Photo by the author.*

Foothill High was located on the west side of Interstate 680, which ran north–south and took many parents south to the rapidly expanding Silicon Valley for work.

About one-fourth of Foothill High students lived on the east side of Interstate 680, specifically in the Valley Trails and Val Vista neighborhoods. The overpasses to get over the freeway were located at Stoneridge Drive to the north and Bernal Avenue to the south. West Las Positas Drive did not have a freeway overpass built until 1985.

For students living in the Valley Trails neighborhood, this meant a 4.6-mile drive (by school bus or car) from their house to campus—a route from Hopyard Road to Stoneridge Drive to Foothill Road. Quickly enough, students figured out a faster way to school that took less than a mile.

"When the school first opened, the kids would come across *over* the freeway," said Keegan, the assistant principal. "The first week or two, the highway patrol came by and said, 'Hey, we have to stop the kids running across the freeway.' We told the kids, 'Don't run across.' But we never said anything about going *underneath*."

A close-up of what the opening to the tunnel looked like. If the water was high, kids would build a bridge to walk over the Creek. *Photo by the author.*

An eight- to ten-foot-high tube went underneath the freeway, big enough to walk through without needing to bend over. It was dark and spooky. You'd hear the cars above you. The only light was from the other end. Drops of water could be heard. It was a badge of courage to walk in the tube under the freeway.

The first time that Tina Faelz discovered this shortcut, she was with her younger brother, Drew.

"We'd go down to the Creek and catch tadpoles every once in awhile," Drew said. "We were right there at the corner where the two creeks met, and she saw some people she knew across at the tunnel. She asked them what they're doing over there. They said, 'It's a shortcut to school.'"

In February or March 1984, Shirley's mother called Steve Faelz and told him that Tina was no longer taking the bus. Faelz met with his adopted daughter after school at Del Freeze on Hopyard Road in the Lucky's Shopping Center. They ate hamburgers and drank milkshakes. Tina cried as she explained the problems she was having on the bus to her dad.

Steve Faelz tried to convince Tina that she needed to take the bus again. He wasn't comfortable with her taking the shortcut under the freeway. Tina explained it was no big deal; all the kids took the shortcut. Steve again urged her to take the bus. Tina made no promises.

"It's one of my big failures in life," Steve Faelz recalled, three decades later. "I didn't pursue that. I didn't go to the school, talk to the teachers or administrators. I feel terrible about that. It's something I've thought about over the years. I've kicked myself a lot and beat myself up over it. It was inexcusable. I'll probably go to the end of my life and always question myself."

Faelz stopped taking the bus to avoid the bullying. Usually, Shirley gave her a ride to school in the morning. But Shirley was often at bars until the early morning and, as a result, didn't always wake up in time to get her daughter to school on time. Tina didn't mind being late because it meant she avoided her bullies before the first class. Due to the frequent tardiness, Tina ended up in detention.

One of the last class assignments that Faelz completed before her death was related to future goals in life. Faelz wrote a four-year plan for all the classes she planned on taking through high school. She wanted to attend the two-year Chabot College, just over the hill in Hayward. For a possible career, she listed actress or real estate broker.

The assignment required her to list fifty things in her bedroom. The first item Tina wrote was a Tom Selleck poster. The second was an Erik Estrada poster. She listed a bed, a dresser, a jewelry box, a penny bank, clothes hung in the closet and clothes on the floor, stuffed animals under her bed, junk behind the stereo, a purse, a picture board, records, tapes, yearbooks, scrapbooks, Ziggy posters, perfumes, a necklace holder, a makeup case, hats hanging on the mirror, a jacket hanging on the bed post, pom-poms, yellow wallpaper, white curtains, powder on the dresser and a desk chair.

Another assignment was to write about a place you'd like to visit one day. Tina chose the state of New York because it was an exciting state. Tina wrote:

> *Many people and big cities and fascinating new things to see. I also love fine things they have there, like beautiful clothes, jewelry and anything you want to buy. Also, many actors and actresses live or are from there. The largest city in New York is New York. The beautiful red rose is the state flower. Its capital is Albany. New York is not just full of big cities, it also has lots of farmland upstate where cows are raised for dairy products.*

In mid-March 1984, Tina Faelz, Stacy Coleman and a few other friends went to the movie theater in Dublin. They saw a double feature: *Footloose* and *Angel*.

"Do you remember the movie *Angel?*" Coleman said. "It was horrible."

But that horrible movie led to one of Coleman's best—and final—memories of her friend. Coleman's mom was late picking the girls up at Mann Theatre, so they climbed onto the roof of the nearby Big Yellow House restaurant.

"Tina kept going, 'I'm Angel, look out!' because there was some stupid scene with Angel and a gun," Coleman said. "It was really funny. We were in hysterics. I laughed so hard. And then I started coughing a lot, and then I threw up all over. I thought that was hysterically funny that we threw up all over the Big Yellow House."

Coleman's mother showed up late to pick up the girls and was unusually protective about the girls sticking together. She made a point of waiting until Tina got inside the house.

"That was weird because my mom wasn't overprotective or paranoid," Coleman said. "That whole thing seemed weird. My mom nagged us all the way back to our house, which wasn't that far. I thought, 'That's so weird that my mom is such a rag about this.' And then two weeks later, Tina was dead."

3
A KID WITH BAD ADHD

He's not normal. Something is wrong with him.
—*Lisa Hall*

DECEMBER 29, 1967-APRIL 4, 1984

Steven John Carlson was born on December 29, 1967, in Bakersfield, California. He was the second of four children for parents John and Sandra. The eldest was Tanya, four years his senior. The youngest were twins Richard and Amy, three years younger. The family called him Steven. Everybody else called him Steve.

"In retrospect, Steven had really bad ADHD [attention deficit/hyperactivity disorder]," Tanya said. "They didn't know that back then. He was just really difficult. He was getting into a lot of trouble. He just didn't have any social skills, really. My mom kept worrying about it. My dad thought he would grow out of it. He could be really annoying."

Tanya recalled her brother tried playing youth baseball. It didn't last long. Steve wasn't very coordinated. He was hit by a pitch once, which tore his thumbnail off, and he never played baseball again. Steve didn't try any other sports or after-school programs during his preteen years.

The Carlsons moved to Pleasanton midway through the 1980–81 school year. They bought a house on Lemonwood Way. It was built in 1969. It was a 1,809-square-foot home with four bedrooms, two and a half baths and a two-car garage. The opposite side of Lemonwood was open fields and wouldn't have houses built for another half decade.

The house had two stories. Steve's bedroom was on the second level, directly above the garage. From his window, Steve had an unobstructed 180-degree view of the activity on his street down below, the construction of new houses and condos in the distance, the high school he would later attend to the left, the Creek to the right and Interstate 680 farther to the right.

The house was located in the Muirwood Meadows neighborhood. This specific housing tract was called Foothill Farms. It was a smaller subdivision built from 1968 to 1970.

The house had a pool in the backyard. It was so close to Foothill High that you could hear the bells indicating the start and end of classes. It was a two-minute walk to the football field, and in the fall, the neighborhood streets were filled with cars for football games on Friday nights.

The move to Pleasanton brought the Carlson family a better quality of life on the surface, but problems were brewing.

"I don't know all of the details," Tanya said. "I know my parents had some problems. Things changed then. Steven was just difficult and created problems. I was gone whenever I could possibly be gone, which I feel bad about. I just disengaged from all that. I don't know what was going on with them, my parents, but I know…it wasn't as happy as it had been up until that point."

Steve's first year as a student in the Pleasanton Unified School District began midway through his sixth grade year at Lydiksen Elementary, located 1.2 miles to the north. Tanya was a sophomore at Foothill High. Richard and Amy were in the fourth grade at Lydiksen.

"First time I met them was pretty memorable actually," said Art Guzman, who lived around the corner. "Me and my neighbor Todd Smith, we were hanging out, playing. Here come these two guys, these two tow-headed guys I've never seen before, and they're running down the street, all crazy-like. They were like Fred and Barney. We're like, 'Who are these guys?' It started right then. That was Steve and Richie."

Art Guzman and Richie Carlson were the same age and became close friends. Steve Carlson and Todd Smith were the same age, two years older, and also became buddies. Guzman thought his childhood was like the movie *The Sandlot*.

"We'd go to the Creek almost every day," Guzman said. "That was our hangout. We'd go on long adventures. We'd take a raft and raft down the

Creek and have to carry the raft all the way back up. We'd catch crawdads. That's all we did. Unfortunately, we got busted one time. We got busted shooting .22s. It was stupid stuff. [The Carlson brothers] were pretty influential. They always got us in trouble."

Steve and Richie were good-looking kids. They were lean, had blond hair and the brightest blue eyes you can imagine, and one neighbor described them as "freakishly strong." For a kid who was awkward socially, the lack of athletic skills didn't help Steve fit in.

"All we did was play sports," said neighbor Tony Fisher, who was two years older than Steve. "The more the merrier. If you can't play sports or you're a troublemaker, we don't want to play with you. That's the kind of guy Steve was—and he wasn't very athletic. It seemed like the rest of the family was normal, and he stood out as the troublemaker of the family."

Fisher recalled a few times that Steve joined in the sports games. "It would always turn into him cheating or something, and we'd kick him out of it," Fisher said. "It was definitely his actions that brought everything that happened to him on himself. He was a little shit. He was just the troublemaker in the neighborhood. He got his butt kicked by all of us, all the time. It wasn't like we sent him to the hospital."

Aaron Rix witnessed the way Carlson was treated by his peers—targeted in confrontations—and why it happened so often.

"Steve was just the quirky kind of guy, always had a little something off to him," Rix said. "He was picked on a lot. I remember a bunch of guys chasing after him on their bikes in Val Vista, screaming that, 'We're going to beat your ass!' He was the kid that you'd be down at the Creek, crawdad hunting, and you'd catch a frog, and he'd stomp on it. I'd ask, 'What did you do that for?' and he said, 'Just because.'"

Rix initially felt empathy toward Carlson. Rix was picked on for his red hair and was once chased out of the gym by dozens of angry classmates. Rix spent time trying to analyze why he wasn't fitting in socially, something Carlson never attempted.

"He would just say oddball stuff," Rix said. "I remember one time he openly said, 'I'd like to fuck your mom.' I can't remember who he said it to, but that guy was going to kill him. 'What did you say? No wonder they want to beat you all the time.' Steve almost seemed like he never learned. It was almost like he was oblivious that everybody else isn't completely weird and creepy. It never sunk into the dude."

WHEN THE FOOTHILL FARMS NEIGHBORHOOD was built in 1968, nothing was around it. The high school didn't even exist until 1973 and didn't have all four classes of students until the '76–77 school year. In the '70s through the mid-'80s, the neighborhood was isolated from the rest of Pleasanton.

It was on the west side of Interstate 680, which offered little mobility. The foothills blocked them to the west. The freeway blocked them to the east. Going south meant navigating the windy and dangerous Foothill Road, and the next neighborhood of kids wasn't close. The only other neighborhood was to the north, called Highland Oaks, which led to the Stoneridge Mall.

The mall opened in 1980, the same year the Carlsons moved to town. JC Penney, Emporium-Capwells and Macy's anchored the mall. It provided a hangout for kids and an identity for Pleasanton. Residents no longer needed to travel into Dublin to go shopping.

The overpass at West Las Positas Boulevard didn't exist. The kids from Foothill Farms could see the sign for the Lucky's grocery store over the freeway. But they couldn't go to Lucky's, see their friends in Val Vista or Valley Trails or go to the popular 7-11 unless they traveled under the freeway into the Creek.

For the adventurous, it was no big deal. For those more timid, it was a barrier. The isolation made the kids more close-knit. Many stayed in touch over the years. Three decades later, some of those kids married other kids from the neighborhood. A handful refused to share their stories about the Carlsons out of neighborhood loyalty.

Parents didn't like that kids went into the Creek. Others reluctantly accepted it. Tanya Carlson enjoyed the quiet solitude and wrote poetry at the Creek. For her younger brother Steve and most other kids, the Creek was the place to smoke cigarettes, chew tobacco, try a little pot, drink alcohol or just have some privacy.

"We were an advanced neighborhood," Guzman said. "We were drinking at an early age. It was not too long after [the Carlsons] moved in that Steve said, 'Hey I've got some weed,' and we smoked our first joint. I never did any other drugs. We would drink. We were young. We made suicides. I said, 'What's a suicide?' They said, 'We raided our parents' cabinet and just poured a little of everything into a bottle and then we drink it.'"

Guzman described Carlson as a hyperactive kid with ADHD who would get violent and into fights but was not a psychopath. Guzman recalled one day that Steve Carlson called him a "beaner," and Guzman lost his temper. Guzman chased Steve around his house in a rage. Later in the day, Steve returned with a baseball bat in hand, ready for a fight. Guzman went into his garage, grabbed an edge trimmer, turned it on and said, "Let's go!"

"I swung the edger at him," Guzman said. "I almost hit him, too. It was pretty close."

Cooler heads prevailed, nobody ever made contact with the bat or power tools and the incident was forgotten.

IN THE FALL OF 1981, Carlson enrolled at Wells Middle School in Dublin. At that time, Pleasanton only had one junior high. It wasn't spacious enough for all the students in the growing city. Foothill Ranch was one of the neighborhoods that had its seventh and eighth graders bussed into Dublin.

Carlson ingratiated himself into the melting pot of students with raunchy comments that were the genesis for the "Creepy Carlson" nickname.

"His jokes were grotesque and crude," said classmate Lorraine Vener, a friend of Tina Faelz. "He was the only one who found them funny. The rest of us would look at him, like I don't see what's so funny about that. That's real gross. He would sit there busting up laughing at himself. He called me a brown whore. I didn't even know what that meant."

The Creepy Carlson nickname was based on his lack of basic social skills. The weirdness led to a visceral reaction, especially among the girls. Steve's hormones were raging out of control, and the lack of a filter led to inappropriate actions with numerous girls.

Steve chased one of his sister Amy's friends, Lisa Weiland, around the pool naked one day. Weiland never told her parents, but her older brothers let Steve know that he would get clobbered if he ever did that again.

Rochelle Williams lived on Muirwood Drive in a house that faced Lemonwood Way, which meant the Carlsons lived six houses away. Williams remembered Carlson frequently just lingering outside her house.

"One day, he was in our house," Williams said. "He went upstairs without me knowing. He opened up the bathroom door and ripped open the shower curtain on my sister. She screamed. He started cracking up and laughing. I walked upstairs and told him, 'Get the hell out of our house!' He was cracking up and wouldn't leave. He was just laughing, 'Ha ha ha,' and then he walked out."

Even Steve's elder sister Tanya was not immune to his inappropriate behavior. Steve once hid inside his sister's bedroom when she took a shower. Then, when Tanya returned to her room and got changed, Steve looked at his sister's unclothed body. Tanya never told her parents because Steve knew she was forcing herself to vomit to stay thin, and he threatened to tell their parents.

In the Wells Middle School 1983 yearbook, a photo shows eighth grader Carlson sitting in the corner of a classroom at a desk with an open book and paper on it. The caption reads, "A RARE MOMENT: Steve Carlson has book and paper for class."

SANDRA CARLSON WAS A STAY-AT-HOME mom who expected her kids to come straight home after school, complete chores and finish homework. It was a good concept, but it rarely worked. Friends recalled they were frequently on restriction.

Despite the expectation that their kids would do chores, friends remember the Carlson house was usually in disarray. The kids would wipe crumbs onto the floor. Rabbits and dogs ran around the house all the time, defecating on the carpet and making messes.

The house had red carpet, and everybody had a waterbed. The family room had a pool table, and the front room was filled with mirrors all over the walls. Friends remember odd food restrictions. The kids couldn't drink milk except at dinner. They couldn't eat snacks without permission.

Amy's friends helped with chores so she could go outside and play. Feeling sorry for the way she was treated, the friends gave some of their own clothes to Amy. Those new clothing items invariably got ruined in the laundry. Some of the other mothers in the neighborhood wondered if Sandra ruined Amy's new clothes on purpose. They felt Sandra was over-controlling. Amy's short haircuts were embarrassing. She wore leggings with holes in them or held together by safety pins. Her clothes were stained or generally unkempt.

Amy's closest friends weren't allowed to spend the night at the Carlson house. (They didn't feel comfortable there anyway.) However, Amy was always welcome at her friends' houses and would go on vacation with her friends' families.

John and Sandra never planned on having four children. They were content having just one child. Steve was not planned. The twins were definitely not planned. As their kids became teenagers, John and Sandra became less interested in actual parenting.

Tanya described the family as "dysfunctional."

John and Sandra were regulars at the Popi Lounge, nicknamed "the Wrinkle Room" for its demographic. This was the same hangout for Tina Faelz's mother, Shirley, although it's not believed the parents ever hung out purposely. The Carlson parents would go bowling one night a week and stay out late drinking. Their bowling night became billiards night for the kids. Even if the twins were on restriction, their friends would come over to shoot pool and raid the parents' cabinets for anything to get a buzz.

After delivering the twins, Sandra's doctor gave her some diet pills to help her lose weight. The pills later became illegal, so she started ordering strong caffeine pills from an advertisement in the *National Enquirer*.

The kids raided the stash of these diet pills, called cross tops. Other street names and types for these pills were white crosses, crisscrosses or black beauties. Popular with truck drivers to help them stay awake, the pills were some type of upper, a stimulant with ephedrine. Whatever was inside, the kids enjoyed the jolt of energy the pills provided. Most likely, these pills were the start of Steve Carlson's experimentation with drugs.

IN THE FALL OF 1983, Steve Carlson enrolled as a freshman at Foothill High. Initially, he tried acclimating himself into normal campus activities. He played on the freshman football team. After years of consistently getting involved in street fights, Carlson and his classmates had an outlet for their aggressive natures.

"I loved it when we played football in high school," classmate and neighbor Todd Smith said. "We got to go head-on-head with pads, and I got to crush him. I remember Coach Sweeney said, 'Whoever hits the hardest hurts the least.' Oh hell yeah, here we go. Carlson said, 'I'm going to eat you for lunch.' I was a little scared. Maybe he knows something? I went at him full speed and dropped him. Carlson said, 'I want another shot at Smith.' I dropped him even harder. He was odd. He liked pain."

Smith and Carlson both played offensive and defensive lineman, so they dueled in practice daily.

"He sucked," Smith said. "He wasn't into it. He was just hoping to get chicks. That's what he told me, 'Chicks like guys in a uniform.' All he wanted to do was get laid. That's all he ever thought about."

Another teammate on the football team, Chris Stovall, recalled that Carlson quit the team before the first game.

Three decades later, Carlson told detectives that he started using marijuana and methamphetamine during his freshman year. In 1983–

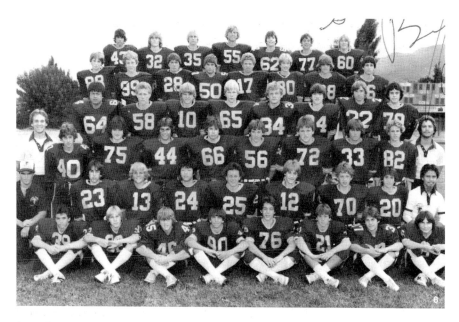

Steve Carlson (65), three rows from the top and fourth from the left, played briefly on the freshman football team in 1983. He quit before the first game, according to a former teammate. *From the Foothill High 1984 yearbook, courtesy of Kevin Wilson.*

84, it wasn't called meth, as we know it now. It was called crank. One of Carlson's quasi-friends sold crank to fellow Foothill High students and was later expelled from the school for dealing.

According to Urban Dictionary:

> *Crank is slang for a low purity, crystallized Methamphetamine that is administered in a powder form. Crank is a stimulant that acts on the central nervous system to increase heart rate and alertness of its users. Highs on the drug last between 8 and 24 hours, and often include a violent "crash" period where the user tends to be prone to aggression. The drug received the nickname "crank" because it was often smuggled in the crank cases of vehicles.*

Carlson's crude behavior and attempts to get laid became more forceful during a tumultuous freshman year. Judy Provost experienced many distressing encounters with Carlson. He often followed her home from school—harmlessly, until one terrifying day.

"Honestly, swear to God, cross my heart on my dad's grave, I thought he was going to rape me," Provost said. "He came into the courtyard. He followed me home, and he was trying to rip my pants off. I was down on the ground. It was dirt. I remember grabbing a tree root and trying to roll myself over because I didn't want him to take my pants off. He was grabbing my boobs and being so aggressive."

Brandie Provost, Judy's younger sister by two years, came home from school in the middle of the attack. "I didn't know what was going on, if he was going to hurt her or rape her or what was going on," Brandie said. "I took my backpack and just started smacking him with it."

Judy Provost continued, "She just started hammering on him. He got up and went to threaten her. Then I got up and went after him. He ran out of the courtyard and that was the end of that. 'Wow' is not even the word. It was super bad. I wouldn't lie or anything. It was horrible. Had it not been for my sister, I really do think, wholeheartedly, that he would have raped me."

GARY HICKLIN TAUGHT INDUSTRIAL ARTS and math at Foothill High during the 1983–84 school year. Faelz was a student in his math class. Carlson was a student in his wood shop class for the fall semester.

"I got along with him," Hicklin said. "He was a crazy, mischievous kid. But those were the kids I liked, that I dealt with. There was no reason not to get along with him. I never had a grudge against him. He tended to be a likeable person to me."

For the 1984 spring semester, the students in wood shop and metal shop switched. The classrooms were next to each other. Hicklin still saw Carlson a lot, practically every day. Carlson didn't get along with metal shop instructor Frank Mueller as well and often came into Hicklin's class to talk about a variety of things.

The location of the metal and wood shops leant itself to being a place where fights took place. It was usually a little pushing and shoving, maybe a few punches. It would end quickly, and everybody was fine. Hicklin broke up fisticuffs so frequently, he said, half-joking, that he never sprinted to break up a fight. Except for one day, around March 1984.

Hicklin heard two boys were getting into it. He left his classroom to break it up, thinking it was just another fight. Soon enough, Hicklin realized this was not just another fight.

"I saw Carlson just unload on this kid," Hicklin said. "It was the most violent, quickest, fastest fight I've ever seen. I sprinted to the fight because I thought he was going to kill him. He was pounding him in the face. It was quite the scene. I got to him, and I broke it up. There was a lot of blood. This was before AIDS issues. I told Carlson, 'Get your ass to the office.' He said he couldn't because he had blood all over him."

Carlson's shirt was torn open. Hicklin ripped the rest of Carlson's shirt off, threw it in Carlson's face and told him to use his shirt as a towel.

"It was as violent a fight as I had ever seen," Hicklin said. "I don't know if [Carlson] went to the office. I was giving first aid to the kid who was beaten badly."

Around the same time, early in 1984, Lisa Hall and Amber Palma went to the Carlsons' house after school one day. Palma was an item with Richie Carlson. All three were attending Wells Middle School. From the moment Hall walked in the door, "Steve was all over me. And, you know, I was a kid. I was like, cool, an older guy likes me."

Hall estimated being inside the house at least ten times. She was inside Carlson's room frequently, described it and remembered being able to see the Creek from his bed. The aggressive behavior wasn't evident right away. But it progressed until, one fateful day, Hall couldn't take it.

"I just remember him telling me that I was going to sleep with him, whether I liked it or not," Hall said. "I remember getting so freaked out. It was things he said, his mannerisms. I remember running down the stairs and saying, 'Amber, let's go.' I never went back over there. I told her, 'Tell Richie to come over here. I don't know what's up with his brother. But let me tell you, he's not normal. Something is wrong with him.'"

4

THE INVESTIGATION BEGINS

Every bizarre motherfucker in the world was coming to light.
—Bill Eastman

APRIL 6-MAY 11, 1984

On the night his sister was murdered, eight-year-old second grader Drew Faelz slept at his best friend Matt Bassett's house, a neighbor who lived on the same court. The next morning, his mother, Shirley, and his father, Steve, came over to get him. They walked Drew to their house at the back of Virgin Islands Court.

"They were divorced for about two to three years at the time," Drew said. "I knew right away something was up because why was my dad at my mom's house? They sat me in the backyard. There was still a ton of family there. They let me know. I didn't believe it. They said Tina is no longer here. I forget exactly how they told me. The first thing I did was go to her room. I opened the door and there were detectives in her room still looking for evidence. Then I got scared."

If Drew Faelz was scared, Steve Faelz was angry. The previous few years had involved a bitter child-custody battle. Steve thought the kids should live with him. He was remarried; held a steady job and had a good source of income; and could provide a better household.

"I always felt that Shirley wasn't running a tight ship," Steve Faelz said. "She had a bunch of roommates to help her pay the bills. She did what she had to do to survive. At the time, I felt she had so many roommates, in and out, it wasn't good for the stability of the household."

Steve was concerned that one of those roommates went crazy, met Tina after school and murdered her. That's what he told the Pleasanton police on the night of the murder. It just made sense to him that one of those guys went crazy.

Police Chief Bill Eastman assigned over half his forty-eight-officer workforce to the murder. "Every bizarre motherfucker in the world was coming to light," Eastman said. "All you had to do was scratch something, and you start coming up with all these people. Like the guy who was at Shirley's house from Santa Rita [Jail] who was talking to the kid."

That would be John Anderson, nicknamed "Recon." Anderson became friends with Shirley's boyfriend, Keith Fitzwater, when they were incarcerated at Santa Rita Jail in Dublin. Anderson fought in the Vietnam War and was known for obsessively talking about his experiences. Anderson drank to excess and was prone to violence when intoxicated.

Police learned that on March 17, 1984, Fitzwater arranged for his friend Anderson and Shirley's friend Penny to meet for drinks. Penny immediately disliked Anderson, who was drinking straight vodka. Anderson yelled at Fitzwater that they were being used. Anderson went inside Tina's room a few times that night and scared her badly. Anderson fell asleep at 5:00 a.m., was asked to leave between 8:00 a.m. and 9:00 a.m. and walked to the Corner House restaurant for breakfast. Anderson charmed a waitress and told her his name was Johnny Diamond. They met at the nearby Pleasanton Sports Park when she got off work and went back to his motel room for part of the night.

Lead Detective Gary Tollefson always thought Faelz knew her killer. At least one dot was connected. Co-workers told police Anderson was late for work the day of the murder. And the next day, he was seen cleaning his knife. Suspicions were raised. However, the evidence never added up that Anderson was responsible.

The biggest reason? He didn't own a car. When police requested Anderson come to the station, he asked for a ride. Detectives felt Anderson was genuinely heartbroken over the death of Faelz. In person, he didn't seem suspicious.

Anderson was an odd guy, and Tina's family was uncomfortable with the time he spent in her bedroom. But he clocked into his job at 3:54 p.m. on the day of the murder. Somebody killing a girl between 3:00 p.m. and 3:15 p.m., cleaning himself up and using public transportation to reach Milpitas in less than an hour was impossible.

INVESTIGATORS TOOK A CLOSE LOOK at Keith Fitzwater. He first met Shirley at the Popi Lounge in Pleasanton when Fitzwater lived in San Ramon. They had been dating about two years. Shirley's family thought Fitzwater was physically abusive to her, but Shirley always denied it. Fitzwater moved into Shirley's bedroom from May to August in 1983 while working for a local electrical contractor as an expediter.

Tina liked Fitzwater at first. She even told close friends she was attracted to him. As time passed, Tina resented Fitzwater because she couldn't spend as much time with her mother when he was around. Fitzwater knew this and moved to Fremont but still slept over two to three nights a week.

On April 3, 1984, Shirley picked up Fitzwater in Fremont and took him back to her house in Pleasanton. They went to the movies, and Shirley drove him home to Fremont. That was the last time Fitzwater saw Tina.

On April 4, 1984, Shirley picked Fitzwater up at work and dropped him off at midnight.

On April 5, 1984, Fitzwater woke up about noon. He took a bus to work at 2:30 p.m., arrived at 2:45 p.m. and used a pay phone a few minutes later to call one of Shirley's friends. He read a newspaper in the break room and then clocked into work at 3:30 p.m. at his new job for a glass company. At 5:30 p.m., Shirley called and told him that Tina was murdered. Fitzwater's boss drove him to the Faelz residence. Fitzwater handed his boss his knife in a sheath and asked him to hold it. Fitzwater later explained it would be improper to be inside the house with the knife, given the manner in which Tina was killed.

The timeline checked out. It wasn't Fitzwater.

DR. THOMAS ROGERS PERFORMED THE autopsy on Tina Faelz's body on April 6, 1984, at the Oakland Coroner's Office at 480 Fourth Street. Rogers dictated his findings into a recording device. His secretary typed up the report. Dr. Rogers took photos of the body, as did Lead Detective Gary Tollefson.

Dr. Rogers collected scalp hair samples, hair from the victim's genitalia, blood samples and smears of vaginal samples. They were placed into evidence at the coroner's office. In all, Dr. Rogers counted forty-four stab wounds and incised wounds on her body. The difference: a stab wound goes deeper with more depth inside; an incise wound is longer on the surface but has less depth beneath the surface.

The body also had a scrape on the right arm, a bruise on the right thigh and three to four scrapes on the forehead; the right side of the head had scrapes as well. Internally, Tina had wounds to her right and left chest.

Bleeding into her chest cavity had defected to her ribs. The conclusion was the victim died from multiple stab wounds and incised wounds, and the individual had a pumping heart when the injuries were sustained.

More than likely, Dr. Rogers concluded, the weapon was a sharp, single-edged weapon with a width of three-fourths to seven-eighths inches or maybe one inch. The length of the blade was three and a half to four inches. Dr. Rogers could not determine if there was more than one weapon. The totality of the stab wounds caused the death more so than one specific fatal blow. Some of the wounds were consistent with defensive wounds. He could not determine if the assailant was left-handed or right-handed, nor could he determine the height or sequencing of the blows. He also could not determine how long it took for those forty-four wounds to be inflicted.

Pleasanton police chief Bill Eastman decided he would not reveal the gory details of the autopsy to a community that was already horrified. Instead, Eastman simply told reporters that Faelz was stabbed over ten times. It would be twenty-eight years before it was publicly known that the real number was forty-four.

On Sunday, April 8, 1984, Officer David Radford transferred all the evidence from the coroner's office back to the Pleasanton Police Department.

As GOSSIP SPREAD THROUGH THE COMMUNITY, some thought the truck driver who first reported the dead body was actually guilty of the murder himself. In order to pinpoint the timeline of the murder and verify the story of the truck driver, Tollefson re-created the route that Larry Lovell took that day.

"Not only did we time it, I took a patrol car and we stopped a trucker," Tollefson said. "I sat down and scooted over as close as I could to the driver to see how much I could see of the [murder] scene. Then I timed the route that he said he took."

Tollefson did exactly what Lovell claimed he did that day. The timing from first spotting a body until making the phone call was fifteen to twenty minutes, depending on the amount of traffic.

Since the 911 call arrived at 3:27 p.m., Lovell must have first spotted the body between 3:07 p.m. and 3:12 p.m. If Weldon Mann was right on time at 3:00 p.m. at the top of Foothill High, he must have seen Faelz alive around 2:55 p.m.

The police used 3:00 p.m.–3:15 p.m. as the window when the murder occurred.

But was the truck driver guilty of the murder and bizarrely alerting police?

"Everybody said the trucker must have done it," Tollefson said. "His time frame worked. We went back and looked at his logs to figure out where he dropped off his loads, like in Pittsburg or Concord. We could re-create his whole day. It checked out. He was just an honest guy who saw something."

ON APRIL 6, 1984, THE DAY AFTER THE MURDER, members of the National Guard and teenage Explorers joined officers in searching the high grass area for the murder weapon. They walked shoulder to shoulder, slowly, through the waist-high grass looking for a knife or any clues. The hours-long search was fruitless.

At Foothill High, Detectives Don Saulsbury, Robert Fracoli and Michael Stewart set up an interview room in the administration building to speak with students and faculty. Principal Roger Dabney, who died a few years later, made an announcement over the speakers that if any students or teachers had any

Shortcut may have cost
Pleasanton student her life

By John Miller
The Tribune

PLEASANTON — Such things do not happen here. Not in Pleasanton.

Children don't get brutally murdered here.

But Tina Faelz, 14, was murdered here Thursday in broad daylight alongside a major freeway only a quarter of a mile from Foothill High School where she was a freshman.

City police said yesterday they have no idea who killed Tina or why. No evidence was found at the crime scene and there are no suspects.

There have been only five murders here since World War II. None of the victims were children.

Even Police Chief William Eastman was shaken by the brutality of the crime. But he was not surprised.

"It can happen anyplace," the straight-talking chief said. "The general tendency for suburban people is to believe that these things don't happen here. But it can happen anywhere."

Eastman said Tina did not appear to have any close friends and apparently felt she was being harrassed by other students, he said.

"She had no confidants and was somewhat of a loner," he said. "There is some indication there has been some harassment," said Eastman, but he ed he didn't consider it of or significance.

... said the strongest theory is

Tina Faelz
Slain near freeway

that somebody hid in the underbrush along a shortcut to the school and attacked Tina before she had a chance to cry out.

Although there are no suspects, Eastman said he has not ruled out that Tina may have known her attacker.

Eastman has ordered half of his 44-member police force to work on the murder investigation.

Yesterday as three detectives interviewed faculty and students and inspected school records for clues, other officers painstakingly searched more than an acre of ground near where Tina's lifeless but still warm body was found in a ditch near a

culvert that runs beneath Interstate 680 just south of the campus.

Despite past warnings from school officials, Foothill students use the culvert as a shortcut to their homes on the east side of the freeway.

Faculty members and students also painted Tina as a loner with few friends who was occasionally picked on or called names by other students.

Principal Roger Dabney said Tina was a "quiet, well-mannered student" and not a troublemaker.

"She appeared to have made a fair adjustment to high school. We are shocked and saddened by Tina's death."

Karen Foster, a sophomore, said students seemed to pick on Tina. "A lot of people hassled her," she said. "I never saw her talking to anyone."

Kathy Sirianni, a sophomore, said she and Tina "used to be really good friends in grade school," but they drifted apart and were not close at Foothill. "Kids used to hassle her on the bus," she said, "until she stopped taking it. She was not really popular."

Stephanie Picard, a junior, said many students "showed a lot of negative feelings" toward Tina for reasons Picard could not really explain.

She said Tina appeared to grow more sullen after her parents separated. "She was a different person," she said. "I guess she had a few problems."

From the April 7, 1984 edition of the *Oakland Tribune*. *From the author's collection.*

information, they should come into the office and talk with the investigators. Stewart talked to sixty-eight different people over the next week.

One of the administrators opened Faelz's locker. Fracoli obtained the contents and logged the items into evidence. The purse obtained the previous day was also logged into evidence with the following items: a comb, Jean Nate perfume talc, powder, eyeliner, lipstick, another eyeliner, mascara, blush or eye shadow, nail polish, pens and pencils, a student ID and a report card dated April 3, 1984.

A major issue for the police was the lack of accurate attendance records for every student. The teachers, to be blunt, were horrible at taking roll.

"That was a problem we had," assistant principal Jack Keegan said. "We didn't know what classes Tina was in that day. We didn't know whether she went to sixth period or fifth period or where was she? The investigators wanted to see the record of every teacher. It was a wakeup call to the way we took attendance. We had to be more accountable."

Through interviews at school, police learned that two or more female students had threatened Faelz at lunch. They learned she was not popular and the frequent target of bullying, although that word wasn't used in 1984. They learned she skipped detention, likely to avoid a confrontation. When school ended, the police questioned Cindy Martini in the principal's office.

"The cops told me they heard that I was her biggest enemy," Martini said. "I was absent that day. I don't remember if I had the flu or if I had an ear infection or what. They asked me where I was and why I was at home and what went on between [Tina] and I, so I told them what happened."

Overwhelmingly, the problems that Faelz had were with other girls, not boys. The idea of another student committing a murder seemed unfathomable.

"I would never expect a high school kid to ever be involved," said Pat Keegan, the wife of Jack Keegan and a teacher at Foothill as well. "That's just not what was going on. Kids were not like that. They had problems. They were mad at each other. It wasn't anything violent."

After school ended, Detective Saulsbury timed how long it would take for somebody to walk from the administration office (at the top of the school) to the crime scene. He measured it at seven minutes and fifteen seconds.

Detective Veteran and other officers returned to the crime scene at about the same time that the murder had occurred the previous day. The officers did a neighborhood canvass, going door to door to see if anybody had seen something the previous day. In his report on the day of the murder, Detective Tollefson noted that some kids were watching the police work from the roof

From the crime scene, the body just below the frame, looking out to the neighborhood, as cops arrive on the scene and residents linger outside. The grass was very high. The Carlson house is on the left. A news helicopter circles overhead. *Courtesy of the Alameda County District Attorney's Office.*

of a house across the street from the crime scene. That was the house of Steve Carlson.

During the neighborhood canvass, Detective Veteran was notified that somebody else had already checked on the house at 7308 Lemonwood Way. At the time, Veteran did not know it was the Carlson house. Veteran and his co-workers contacted a lot of people and chased a lot of leads. None of it led to a suspect.

Police Chief Bill Eastman told reporters, for the next morning's newspaper, that two major leads were checked and turned out to be of no value. Eastman said the two separate people they were seeking—a hitchhiker and a student with a blue backpack—were both located. Neither was a suspect or able to provide any clues to the killing.

The identity of the student with the blue backpack is unknown, but it was not Steve Carlson. However, the police were suspicious of the student's movements and followed up on three occasions in the next week. That student first told police he stayed after school until 3:00 p.m. on the day of the murder, but a teacher and another student thought he left by 2:45 p.m. The student used the catwalk at the West Las Positas overcrossing, which was under construction, to get over Interstate 680. He walked to Donlon Elementary to pick up his sister. She wasn't there. He went home, and his mother was angry that he was late getting his sister. He went to work at a pizza parlor and clocked into work just after 5:00 p.m.

In a follow-up, police said they heard he owned knives. The student removed a small pocketknife from his pocket. Police noticed a cut on the student's hand. During the first interview on April 6, he explained that a pan slipped from his grip at work and cut his finger. When re-interviewed on April 9, the student said he cut his finger at work trying to put a vent cover back in place and it slipped. Detective Saulsbury asked the supervisor at the pizza parlor to show him the location. He inspected it and noted there were edges that could have cut him.

Police heard from other students that the young man was acting strangely. He was usually quiet but had been "antsy" that week at school. On April 10, police went to the student's house to obtain his pocketknife and a larger knife that was in a sheath. The knives were seized, placed into evidence and later tested. Police interviewed the mother, and she said her son had arrived home about 3:40 p.m. on the day of the murder. She gave the officers permission to search his room. They looked at his blue backpack, the army jacket he was known to wear almost daily, his shirt that day and his tennis shoes.

None of the items had blood or anything suspicious on them. The knives were later returned to the family.

DURING THE SCHOOL INTERVIEWS, police also learned that Steve Carlson had been excused from school on the day of the murder due to being sick but was seen on campus intoxicated and locked in a dumpster. The police heard that a group of boys, including Carlson, were drinking alcohol at a house near the crime scene.

On Saturday, April 7, 1984, Carlson came to the police department. It was the first time police interviewed him. Police did not drive him to the station. No record indicates how Carlson got there.

Detective Don Saulsbury led the interview. Saulsbury did not notice any cuts on Carlson's hands. (Saulsbury did note cuts on the hands of Eric Voellm two days earlier.) Saulsbury also did not make note of anything unusual about Carlson's demeanor. The interview lasted thirty minutes. Carlson left the station on his own.

At 1:00 p.m., Sergeant Michael Stewart talked to Katie Kelly, who was in a schoolgirl fight with her close friend Faelz. Kelly's parents were present.

The interview took place at the Kellys' house, the same street on which Faelz had lived.

About 7:00 p.m. that night, Detective Fracoli returned a phone call to Keegan, the assistant principal. Keegan told Fracoli that he saw Carlson on campus between 12:30 p.m. and 12:40 p.m., even though he was supposed to be home sick.

On Wednesday, April 11, 1984, Detectives Bob Fracoli and Don Saulsbury met with Carlson for a second time. They talked for forty-five to sixty minutes. Fracoli noted that Carlson was cooperative, and his behavior was not unusual. The meeting began at Foothill High, where Carlson and Todd Smith were called into the administration building toward the end of the school day.

This is the timeline that Carlson gave police for his actions that day:

- 7:15 a.m.—Arrived at school at usual time, met with several friends, told them his parents were out of town and he was having a party. Could not convince them to cut school with him.
- 7:45 a.m.—Walked home rather than attending first period.
- 8:05 a.m.—Took his mom's car and drove to the south parking lot at Foothill. Picked up three boys he knew and drove them to his house. They drank beer, vodka and Jim Beam.
- 8:20 a.m.—Two of the boys left the Carlson home so they would not be late for their next class.
- 8:50 a.m.—Carlson and the other boy returned to school. They went to the wood shop room, the class of the other boy. Wood shop teacher Gary Hicklin told Carlson to get to his own class. Carlson headed for the parking lot. Near the mobile home by the parking lot, two other boys grabbed Carlson, put him in a garbage dumpster and locked him in there for ten minutes. Carlson then went home, ate a hamburger and watched TV.
- Carlson then said he went back to school and waited for the bell to ring ending third period but did not see his friends. He went home and fell asleep. When he woke up, he drove his mom's car around the Muirwood area. When he returned home, it was lunch and three of his friends had let themselves into his house. Carlson told them to get out.
- Five minutes later, two other boys and a girl showed up at his house.
- 12:20 p.m.—The girl left so she would not be tardy. The other two boys went for a ride in Carlson's mom's car. The car was smoking badly, so they returned home.

- The three boys walked back to school. They were fifteen minutes late for fifth period. Carlson's teacher said he was listed as sick that day and told him to go home, which he did for the rest of the day.
- After school, Carlson said Todd Smith came to his house. He wasn't sure of the time. They drove in Carlson's mom's car again. He described a wide variety of locations they went in the neighborhood, including Muirwood Drive, which they traveled along at sixty miles per hour.
- Carlson said they saw Tina walking through the hole in the fence of the football field. She gave them a disapproving look, which Carlson interpreted as "you're dumb to be driving" because most students knew Carlson did not have a license. Carlson said he was positive it was Tina.
- Carlson said he dropped off Todd Smith to get his books, returned his mom's car to the driveway and locked the car. Then he saw Smith and Weldon Mann. They talked a few moments and Mann said he had to leave.
- Then Smith showed Carlson how to ride his moped. They took turns riding the moped, along with Smith's younger brother, and they drove the moped around the neighborhood. They were riding northbound on Ashwood approaching Lemonwood when Eric Voellm and Jay Dallimore jumped in front of them, almost causing them to crash. The boys said, "There is a dead dude in the field."
- Carlson said he went down the path to the body, did not think it was Tina, ran home, telephoned his grandmother and saw out his window that police were coming.

It should be noted that Carlson's timeline is similar to but does not exactly match what others have provided. It's unknown which movements are true, partially true or false. His version of events is printed for context, not for historical accuracy. Most importantly, none of the five students who were interviewed at the crime scene said Carlson was with them.

The detectives drove Carlson and Smith to a handful of locations in their neighborhood and near the crime scene, trying to pinpoint their various locations on the day of the murder and the time it would take to get from one place to the next. It lasted about thirty minutes. Once again, no cuts were noticed—or included in the report—and the boys were let go.

On Tuesday, April 17, 1984, Detective Saulsbury talked with Todd Smith. This was the third time police interviewed Smith, due to the inconsistencies in his previous two statements.

"They were making me feel like I was the guy who did it," Smith said in an interview. "They said, 'If you come clean now, nothing will happen to you. This will come off your record. You're only fifteen. You can tell us what happened.' [I would respond,] 'I didn't do it.' Why are you even talking to me without my parents?"

Within the next day or two, Gary Smith, the father of Todd and the building inspector in the city of Pleasanton, confronted Police Chief Eastman to leave his son alone on the investigation. Eastman's response to Gary Smith was, "We're running a murder investigation. We're going to talk to anybody we want to talk to on it. Doesn't mean they have to talk with us. But get off my back on this one."

AMONG STUDENTS, THE SUSPICION OF Steve Carlson's possible involvement was nearly immediate. Even after the story faded from the newspaper, the suspicions did not go away. The students were already whispering about whether Carlson was involved. Then, incredibly, it was Carlson's own mouth that sealed their assumptions.

"I was at a party like two days after all that went down," said classmate Jeff Wainwright. "I think it was one of the Chargin [twins]. We were at the party. And they said Carlson just admitted to killing her. Nobody was in shock. Everybody kinda knew it."

The opinion within the police department was mixed on a profile of the killer. Most thought Faelz knew her attacker, at least superficially, because no evidence existed that she was trying to flee. But most didn't think a student could really be capable of such a violent crime.

"It's tough too because when [Carlson] says these things, if he says this to three people, eighty-five know about it and claim they said it to him," Eastman said. "It takes us in so many directions."

It wasn't just the students. Even teachers were suspicious.

Gary Hicklin, the wood shop teacher who knew Carlson better than any other adult on campus, immediately had a bad gut feeling about Carlson. Hicklin had seen Carlson's rage in a vicious bloody fight two months before. Hicklin unlocked Carlson from a dumpster on the day of the murder. The night after the murder, Hicklin couldn't sleep, talking to his wife through the night about this uneasy feeling he had that Carlson was somehow involved in the death.

During the on-campus memorial, held four days after the murder, Hicklin kept his eyes locked on Carlson the entire time.

"I can tell you exactly where he was," Hicklin said. "He was off to the right by the bathroom. He stood next to the Chargin brothers [twins John and David]. Tina's parents were in the front. I thought there's no way he did this. His attitude and what was going on and everything, nobody could have done that. He couldn't have acted that way at a memorial."

Hicklin was torn. He didn't think a student was capable of stabbing another student to death. Yet he couldn't help but wonder if Carlson was involved in some way.

A few days after the memorial, Carlson walked into Hicklin's classroom to talk between periods. This wasn't uncommon. Carlson felt more comfortable with Hicklin than any other teacher and would talk to him frequently.

"I'll always remember this," Hicklin said. "He came through the door. He was on my right. We went to the side. We sat and talked. I asked him, 'Did you kill Tina?' And that's when he said, 'Only God knows.' The look on his face and his body language—that's what haunted me forever."

Not wanting to forget any details, Hicklin documented all of his interactions with Carlson. Hicklin typed two full pages of notes onto his AppleWorks computer and saved the notes on a floppy disc. The notes included the eerie conversation, the vicious fight and other odd behaviors. (That floppy disc was lost over the years, and all the evidence is gone.)

Hicklin couldn't stop thinking about Carlson. He talked with his wife and other teachers. They discussed if Hicklin should tell the police. Hicklin ended up telling Assistant Principal Keegan about the conversation and fight. Keegan assured Hicklin that he would tell the police.

"If I look back on Carlson from the beginning, I don't think he was a monster," Hicklin reflected. "I don't think he was a crazy kid who would do this. When I told Jack what happened, we didn't know she was stabbed forty-four times. In Jack's defense, there's no way you thought a kid would do that. You knew he was a problem child—and that's my perspective as a teacher. There was no way this kid could do that. He was a relatively nice kid. I had him that first semester. He was the Eddie Haskill type. He wasn't a bad kid at all."

THE FOLLOWING WEEK, APRIL 16 TO 20, was spring break. Campus was closed. When school returned, Keegan called a staff meeting and advised his teachers to pay closer attention than usual. People might start acting strange after Faelz's murder. Observe critically. Take notes. If you see something unusual, report it.

Sue Klas, a physical education teacher, noticed that one of her students was acting unusual. Klas wrote a letter that was received by Edith Stock, another assistant principal, on May 2, 1984.

Klas wrote that Steve Carlson had always been a weird kid. But since returning from spring break, Carlson had really gone downhill. Carlson isolated himself from the rest of the class and stopped all participation. Klas listed examples of his non-participation, expressed her concern and asked what she should do. It isn't known what became of Klas's concerned note or how seriously it was taken.

Meanwhile, neighborhood kids continued to play amateur detectives. Tony Fisher and his friends had a suspicion that Carlson was responsible. They didn't know for sure and didn't have any evidence. Fisher was a senior, lived around the corner from Carlson, wasn't intimidated by him and had even roughed him up a few times. Fisher confronted Carlson on his lawn a few days after the murder. It was an uncomfortable talk.

"I remember asking him, giving him the third degree, 'Where were you?' and asking in a way where I thought he did it," Fisher said. "I remember leaving that conversation unsure and maybe even leaning toward he didn't. Just by his reactions. He was too calm. He had an answer for everything. He's either a very good liar or he didn't do it. I went away, in the back of my mind still suspicious but not knowing for sure. I didn't want to accuse him and think he did, if he didn't do it."

Matt Sweeney was a first-year teacher at Foothill High who taught civics and economics to seniors and coached Carlson on the freshman football team.

"Carlson was socially awkward," Sweeney said. "The other kids definitely made fun of him. He got along with me. Even his so-called friends made fun of him. The fact that the police didn't pin it on him right out of the gate, I always felt it was a bad rumor, and it wasn't fair to Carlson."

Eddie Gallagher was four years older and no longer attended Foothill High. He observed Carlson getting called "murderer" by other kids as he walked by and was one of the few who defended Carlson.

"He wasn't creepy [to me]," Gallagher said. "He was just a dorky kid. He smoked pot, but I never saw him do anything else. I felt sorry for him because the other kids picked on him. When it happened, everyone was saying this stuff to him. I stuck up for him. I didn't think it was right. Nobody knew what the hell happened. Nobody knew anything."

The rumors didn't go away because of Carlson's own mouth. The lingering question is whether Carlson was cajoled into these so-called confessions, using Faelz's death to establish himself as a badass, or if he just couldn't help himself.

"It wasn't immediate, but it definitely didn't take long," said Art Guzman, a neighbor and close friend of Steve's younger brother Richie. "When we'd be hanging out, partying, Steve would get drunk, and he would say, 'I did it.' Then he'd say, 'I'm just kidding.' We'd think, 'You're not kidding. I bet you did it.' Then he'd say, 'No, I didn't.' Then it would happen again.

"Everybody felt like, 'Yeah, I don't think anybody else could have done it.' It had to be him. It's not based on any evidence, except that he used to say he did it. I knew the guy well. I knew when he was bullshitting or being truthful. He was being truthful when he said, 'I did it,' and he was being a bullshitter when he said, 'Nahh, I'm just kidding.'"

ON FRIDAY, APRIL 13, 1984, police videotaped the crime scene and surrounding area between 12:45 p.m. and 2:00 p.m. They videotaped the crime scene again four days later. On Saturday, April 14, 1984, the reward for information leading to an arrest was up to $13,050 and would eventually reach $25,000—including $5,000 from Steve Faelz and $1,000 from Chief Eastman.

Lead Detective Gary Tollefson enlisted the help of the East Bay Parks and Recreation Department to fly above the crime scene in a two-seat helicopter.

People v. Carlson 170014

An aerial view, looking east, of the crime scene. One of the 911 calls was made from the house on the right with the pickup truck out front. The Carlson home is on the corner where the streets converge. *Courtesy of the Alameda County District Attorney's Office.*

An aerial view, looking south, of the crime scene. Truck driver Larry Lovall pulled to the right side of the highway to view what he thought was an injured girl. Lovall then drove to the Pleasanton Fairgrounds to call for help. *Courtesy of the Alameda County District Attorney's Office.*

Tollefson took aerial photos of the crime scene, neighborhood, campus and Interstate 680.

Over 150 people had been interviewed—teachers, students, administrators, neighbors, family acquaintances and workers from a nearby construction site. Some were questioned two to three times. The tall weeds in that area were searched twice with metal detectors. No weapon was found.

Police Chief Bill Eastman told the *Valley Times* there were still more leads to follow. Up to twenty-four police employees were working on the case that week. The cops were pulling twelve- to sixteen-hour shifts. "Most of our time has been spent interviewing and chasing blind leads," the *Times* quoted Eastman. "We all wake up with ideas at one and two in the morning."

Eastman told the press his theory was that Faelz knew her killer—perhaps they were only acquaintances, but they were not total strangers. Eastman admitted he was still puzzled about the motive for the killing. She was not sexually assaulted, and nothing was stolen. It didn't appear to be a drug deal gone awry.

People v.
Carlson
170014

An aerial view, looking west, with the Valley Trails neighborhood at the bottom of the photo and the Foothill High campus at the top. Construction of new homes was to the left of campus. The open fields to the right of the crime scene became houses a few years later. *Courtesy of the Alameda County District Attorney's Office.*

One of the local newspapers offered a psychic to assist. "Why not?" thought Eastman. The police chief caught some flak from inside his own department. Eastman told the naysayer, "Then solve the fucking case."

In retirement, Eastman leaned back in his chair, rubbed his beard and said with a smile, "Why not listen? It could be pure mythical bullshit. But what if it triggers your thought in one area, and then you start finding more and more? You've checked everything else. Why not?"

IN LATE APRIL 1984, PLEASANTON POLICE thought they finally had a break in the case, involving a twenty-three-year-old man named Walter Nyman.

On April 10, 1984, five days after Faelz's murder, a sixteen-year-old female was walking home from a bus stop in Felton, which is about eight miles north of Santa Cruz. She walked across a covered bridge and saw a two-door Oldsmobile drive past her, pull over and then stop. A white male got out of the car and was drinking a beer. As the girl walked toward the male, he yelled at some nearby boys in an angry voice and scared them away.

Nyman put his beer down, grabbed the girl, put his hands over her nose and mouth and told her not to scream or he would kill her. Nyman unzipped her white work shirt and started fondling her breasts. He said if she kissed him, he would let her go. She complied, hoping he would leave. Nyman walked the victim to the other side of the bridge and down a trail that led to a brush. As he tried to pull her into the brush, the girl slipped out of her jacket and ran away, leaving her jacket and purse.

The girl ran home, called 911 and returned to the area with her boyfriend to look for the suspect. He was gone but had left her jacket and purse with nothing missing. The police found his Michelob beer bottle and tested it for fingerprints. The two boys at whom the suspect yelled were located and said they saw the suspect drive away.

On April 11, the victim located the suspect and his car at Henry State Park. He drove away, but she got his license plate number. On April 23, the vehicle was stopped by a Scotts Valley police officer for speeding. They determined it was the car they were seeking in the attempted rape. The driver was Walter Nyman. Initially, Nyman denied any involvement and consented to his car being searched.

A few days later, detectives contacted Nyman again. His fingerprints matched those on the beer bottle, and he was wearing the same hat the victim had described. He also had a tattoo on his upper right arm that matched the description the victim had given. Nyman was arrested and booked into Santa Cruz County Jail.

Because of the similarities of a tunnel (or drainage ditch), Nyman became a person of interest in the Faelz investigation. Nyman's grandmother told Pleasanton police that Nyman had been living in Pleasanton. Then, on the night of April 5, 1984, Nyman showed up at his grandmother's house in Felton, out of the blue, with few belongings and visibly upset about how his life was going.

Not enough evidence existed to eliminate Nyman or charge him with the crime. However, he remained the most significant "person of interest" in the case.

On May 8 and 9, 1984, city workers from Pleasanton worked with police officers and detectives on the crime scene and the vast open fields around it. They cut back branches, mowed down the grass and canvassed the area again. No murder weapon or helpful clues were found.

On May 11, 1984, Detective Gary Tollefson delivered evidence to be analyzed by Theresa Spear, a criminalist for the Alameda County Sheriff's Crime Lab. It was still seven years before DNA was used by law enforcement, but Spear was on the cutting edge of examining blood and other trace evidence. Spear looked for the presence of semen on Faelz. She made small cuts into the crotch of Faelz's underwear and ran tests. No spermatozoa was found.

Faelz's blood sample was provided in a sealed glass vial. Spear performed ABO typing and a blood typing called enzyme typing. The blood cells had been hemolyzed, meaning they had been broken apart, so the test used for the ABO sample could not be used.

Spear also examined Faelz's blood-soaked clothing for trace evidence like fibers or hair. The victim's shoes and fingernail clippings were tested. The dry material found on Faelz's abdomen was tested for sperm. The testing produced no leads, no evidence, no suspects and no answers.

5

A COMMUNITY MOURNS

I was always the kid whose sister got killed. I always felt whispers.
—*Drew Faelz*

APRIL 6-JUNE 30, 1984

In a world without Internet, Facebook, Twitter and twenty-four-hour news channels, not everybody heard the news of Tina Faelz's murder the day it happened. Either somebody called you or you happened to be in front of a television for the local news at 6:00 p.m. or 11:00 p.m.

For most people, they learned the next day. Lisa Celestre's mom, Diane Jones, had spent the bulk of the previous night at the house of her friend and co-worker Shirley Faelz. Jones came home late that night, after her daughter was asleep. The next morning, she went into her daughter's room to deliver the heart-wrenching news.

"I had a chair sitting next to my bed," remembered Celestre. "I was totally into *Circus* magazines. I loved my hair bands. I'd just bought that magazine the day before. My mom comes in and sits on my brand-new magazine, and I was pissed. I'm thinking, 'Why are you sitting on my magazine?' But I could tell she was upset. She was crying. She said Tina was hurt, and she died. She didn't really say stabbed. You don't find a lot of fourteen-year-old kids reading the newspapers. But I started reading the stories, and that's when I read the details on it."

Lorraine Vener, who once fell out of a tree after trying Skoal with her friend Tina, was getting ready for school when her mother asked her to get the newspaper off the front porch. Vener saw the headline and started screaming.

"Tina's name just popped out at me in the article," she said. "My mom came into the kitchen. I showed her the paper. She knew Tina. Tina had come over to the house, and my mom made us peanut butter sandwiches. We sat down at the kitchen table, and she started crying. She called my dad, who was already at work. I think it was an hour later that I finally went to school. The neighbor took me. Everybody was walking around the campus in a daze. It was shock and awe for a long time. Even to this day, even talking about it right now, I still feel the exact same thing."

Nearly three thousand miles away, the Foothill High marching band was at the end of a weeklong field trip in Orlando, Florida, for a number of performances. Freshman Mariha Bowers was in a hotel room when a friend came to the door and asked if she knew a girl named Tina Staples. Bowers used a payphone to confirm it was her friend Tina Faelz who had been killed.

Bowers still performed with the rest of the band. "The band moms were like, 'Jeez, Mariha, we could cut your legs off, and you'd still go out there and march,'" Bowers said. "What else could I do? I didn't want to be by myself."

Sophomores Karen Foster and Kathy Sirianni did something they quickly regretted. Sirianni was a neighbor and one of the girls who threw rocks at Faelz earlier in the day that she was killed.

"We were young and impetuous and wanted to do something," Foster said. "We brought flowers over to Tina's mom a couple days after this happened. Our heart was in the right place. But we didn't have the maturity level to know that wasn't a good idea. We went in, and I remember that her mother was there. I don't know if she was in shock or sedated or both. I remember the house was very dark. Another man was there. He took the flowers and said, 'Thank you very much.' I remember thinking about that afterward. I felt like we were torturing them. We didn't know her family well enough to do that."

Sirianni added, "I remember after it happened telling police officers that we threw rocks at her. I still feel that guilt. I can't change it. I don't know what I can tell myself. It was wrong. I'll never forget those purple lavender pants she had on that day."

Feelings of guilt and shame hung over the girls who had bullied Faelz. Over the next three decades, the guilty conscious remained. On October 8, 2011, Rachael Scarlett sent this author the following e-mail:

I am truly ashamed about what I can tell you regarding my interactions with Tina. It is one of the few things I've done in my life I truly and sincerely regret. I have shared this experience with many people but especially younger generations in hopes they can learn a valuable lesson about teasing other kids and how wrong it is. Earlier the day Tina was stabbed to death, myself and one of my best friends, Kathy Sirianni, teased her while walking back from lunch. I really had no interaction with Tina except for this horrible day. My friend Kathy lived on the same street as Tina and did not like her one bit, why I am not sure of. We threw rocks at her and called her Tuna as we did it. We found out I believe the next day at school and what we did began to sink in. We were questioned by police and told them everything we knew. I am ashamed that I was part of making Tina's last day on this earth a terrible one and I hope this helps you in some way.

Rachael Scarlett wasn't the only person feeling shame. About eight hundred miles north in Washington, Tina's biological father, Ron Penix, found out his daughter had been murdered from his mother.

"I've never gotten over Tina," Penix said. "I feel guilt-ridden that if we'd stayed together, Tina would still be alive. But you can't change the past. I was just lost, to say the least. What do you do? You pray and ask for forgiveness."

Custodian Vince LaRosa arrived at school earlier than usual on Monday, April 9, 1984, to make sure there was hot coffee in the teachers' lounge and then set up tables and chairs outside the cafeteria for a memorial to a girl whom most people on campus didn't know existed.

"I remember little bits of the memorial," Bowers said. "My friends reading their poems, and they were crying so hard nobody could understand them."

Freshman Kim Scola told the assembly how she became friends with Tina when she moved to the Pleasanton area a few years earlier. They provided moral support to each other during awkward junior high dances and an arduous freshman year. "We will all miss you," Scola said. "I'm sure you're in a better world today, where the skies are always blue."

Student body president Jim Butler announced the school would plant a lilac tree in Faelz's honor. "It will bloom every year at this time, to remind us of Tina."

They played the song "Stop Dragging My Heart Around" by Stevie Nicks—Tina's favorite song. "Every time I hear that song, I get chills and think of her—every single time," said friend Becky Tantillo. "It's a kick-ass song."

Funeral is held for Tina Faelz, 14, student stabbed in drainage ditch

APR 1 0 1984

By John Miller
The Tribune

CASTRO VALLEY — Funeral services were held yesterday for Tina Faelz, the 14-year-old Pleasanton high school student who was found fatally stabbed in a drainage ditch along I-680 last Thursday.

The slaying sent shock waves through the community and through Foothill High School, where Tina was a student. Reward money for information leading to the arrest of the killer has reached $7,000, including a $1,000 contribution from Police Chief William Eastman, whose two daughters also attend Foothill.

Tina's body was cremated and her ashes were scattered over Yosemite National Park.

Several students attended funeral services at Chapel of the Valley, and two of them, Kim Scola and Kristin Hendershott,

read poems in memory of Tina. Earlier in the day, Foothill High school freshman class president Mark Pendleton led students in a memorial service at the school.

Tina is survived by her parents, Shirley and Steven Faelz; a younger brother, Drew Faelz; and her grandparents, Lee and Corrine Faelz and Richard and Alfreda Griffiths.

Eastman yesterday reported no new leads or suspects in the baffling case. He said the motive remains a mystery.

"We have no new developments and nothing that I would call a suspect at this point," Eastman said. "We are talking to a couple of people we are curious about, but I couldn't label them as suspects. We're just trying to iron out some inconsistencies in some of their statements."

Police have interviewed numerous students, including some

who reportedly had argued with Tina on a school bus about a month ago. Eastman said police also re-inspected the drainage ditch and an adjacent field, hoping to turn up some evidence, but found nothing.

Eastman said police want to talk to anybody who may have seen anything suspicious near the still-unfinished Las Positas overcrossing of I-680 north of the school or near the drainage culvert where it passes under the freeway south of the campus. Tina and other students used the culvert, which is big enough to walk through, to reach the east side of the freeway.

Contributions to the reward fund may be sent to the Pleasanton Police Department. Persons who wish to give information anonymously to the "secret witness" program may call 455-4661. They are not required to leave their names or to testify in court.

From the April 10, 1984 edition of the *Oakland Tribune. From the author's collection.*

One more incident stands out from the memorial. Whether it was an innocent mistake or a hideous joke, it's telling about the culture at Foothill High at the time. In the middle of the memorial, a song was played over the school's public address system. Not just any song either. It was the chorus from the Queen song "Another One Bites the Dust."

The funeral was held later that day in Castro Valley. A group of Faelz's friends gathered at a café close to the church before the service.

"We were laughing and telling stories about how funny she was and remembering all the fun things," Bowers said. "We thought we were going to be OK. Everybody broke down at the funeral."

A lot of Tina's friends couldn't bring themselves to walk up to the open casket solo. Stacy Coleman was somewhat the ringleader. Although the same age, Coleman was the rock for the teenage girls to lean on. Coleman ended up walking six different girls to the open casket, so she observed Tina's body in the casket more than anybody.

Above: The family chose to spread Tina's ashes at Yosemite National Park in 1984. Drew is on the left with his mother and father. *Courtesy of Karin Reiff.*

Right: Tina's ashes were buried under a tree close to this waterfall. *Courtesy of Karin Reiff.*

"She was wearing a gray dress that was probably polyester but supposed to look like raw silk," Coleman said. "It was real light. It was a high collar. Her hair was hideous. She had it straight across that came into bangs and then like a matronly hairdo. It was nothing Tina would ever pick for her own hair. She was laid out and her hands were folded over [across her chest]. Her fingernails had chipped-up red polish. That upset me really bad that they didn't either take it off or paint over or do something. She had a lot of little scratches all over her hands. I don't know what was done to her face, I don't know if it was from where she fell, but you could see the wax they put on her skin to fill in [the cuts]."

The family elected to have Tina's body cremated. They went to Yosemite National Park and spread her ashes under a tree.

ONE WEEK AFTER THE FUNERAL, it was spring break. The frequency of stories in the newspapers faded from the front page to the inside pages and then disappeared. There wasn't news to report. The police had no fresh leads or suspects. When students returned from spring break, it was back to normal for most of the campus. Thoughts turned to the junior prom and the senior ball and the countdown to graduation and summer break. For Tina's closest friends, she remained fresh on their minds.

"I remember on the last day of school, her typing folder was still there," Bowers said. "I took it, just to have something of hers."

Katie Kelly, the best friend who was in a fight with Tina at the time of her murder, continued going to school. She was there physically but never there mentally.

"After that, I failed all my classes," Kelly said. "They put me in remedial English. They didn't equate—maybe she's depressed? I saw a guidance counselor. She said, 'Maybe you need a vacation?' A month later, I went back and she said, 'Did you have your vacation?' I said no."

For Eric Voellm, one of the students who discovered the body, getting the image of a bloody, dead classmate out of his mind was impossible. Voellm's father worked at the same company as classmate Martine Burnham's mother. A couple weeks after the murder, the families gathered to discuss the circumstances.

"My mom thought Eric needed counseling because it was pretty gruesome," Burnham said. "He didn't go into a lot of the details. I know it was pretty bloody. I know he stabbed her multiple times. I heard, at one point, he cut her fingertips off. I don't know if that's true or not."

It was not true about her fingertips getting cut off, but that gives an indication of the rumors spreading around campus.

Sean West, the neighbor walking behind Faelz that fateful day, couldn't avoid a perpetual reminder because his upstairs bedroom overlooked Faelz's house.

"I looked over there all the time and wondered what her life would be like," West said. "Tina had a hard time. Socially, she didn't really fit into a lot of places. She lived a sad life. That's the hardest part of all. She never got the opportunity to gain some momentum with school and socially. The other girls picked on her, and I don't know why."

For freshman Joy Erven, every visit to her locker was a reminder of her slain classmate. "Her locker was underneath mine," Erven said. "It was chilling to have it right there. It was alphabetical. It's Erven-Faelz everywhere. In the classes I had with her, because I remember one in particular, she sat behind me. It was really scary. We thought that people were going to murder us in our beds. Usually, when somebody transfers in, they assign that locker. They left hers empty the rest of the year."

Faelz even took on a mythical presence in the Valley Trails neighborhood.

"I was driving around one night, and all of a sudden, a streetlight across the street from our house went out," said Dan Carleton, a parent who lived on the same street as the Faelzes. "My daughter Jackie said, 'Oh, Tina is around.' It wasn't just Jackie. It was other friends, too. They would notice that streetlight going out, and they felt like Tina was around. I didn't pursue that conversation."

Since the seventh grade, Katie Kelly and her friend Tina Faelz had been subjected to threats and taunts by bullies at school, at the bus stop and in her neighborhood. Swiftly, the attention she received was the opposite.

"People who were once really awful to me were really nice to me," Kelly said. "Sherry Jones took me aside in the library. She wanted to let me know how sorry she was. Jeannie House was another one. She wrote this really nice apologetic note in my yearbook. It's really interesting when you compare the yearbook notes from the eighth grade to the ninth grade. In the eighth grade it was, 'Katie, you're so nice. We'd hang out with you…if you weren't friends with Tina.' They were putting this condition on our friendship. Then the next year, 'Oh, we're so sorry about Tina.' That's a very sad commentary."

The next time Tina Faelz's name was a big discussion around Foothill is when yearbooks arrived the final week of the school year. Yearbooks are notorious for students sneaking inappropriate comments without the adviser noticing. They're usually harmless. That annual was filled with questionable content.

The seniors were asked to predict where they would be in ten years. Three answers went beyond misguided crassness. Ed Arbacauskas wrote, "pushing troops through the jungles of El Salvador with M-16 at my side." Joel Cacia said, "I want to be president of the American Nazi party." Michael DeSantis topped them with his entry: "In ten years, I will be in jail for rape and murder." (By 1994, he wasn't in jail. But by 2001, he was dead.)

The first time Tina appeared in the yearbook was on page 180, when the freshman photos begin. In the middle of the page, at the top, is a photo of Tina, Katie Kelly and Kim Bethune. The photo was taken during freshman orientation. Faelz is on the far left of the photo, her purse in her right hand, and she's pointing with her left hand to the parking lot. Half of her mom's car is in the right side of the photo, and the front door is open.

The caption reads, "Bye mom, I'll be OK."

The caption doesn't identify the students. Most didn't even realize Tina was in the photo. For those who did recognize Tina, they were appalled at the caption and felt salt was poured in their wounds. They felt somebody on the yearbook staff was part of those who made her life miserable. Some took it even further, launching a conspiracy theory that somebody from the yearbook staff was involved in Tina's death.

In truth, the caption was a guiltless victim of yearbook deadlines. This author took journalism classes inside the same classroom as the yearbook staff. Their deadlines were all over the room, and a lasting memory was how early they were. For a page early in the yearbook about freshman orientation, it was probably completed in October and shipped off to the printer long before April 5.

If the caption wasn't caught during the final proofreading, it's almost assuredly because yearbook staffs are overwhelmingly seniors and juniors; nobody from the yearbook staff knew her, and they didn't even realize she was in that photo.

A less virtuous mistake can be found on page 195. It's a full-page memorial with trees and a rainbow. Faelz's freshman class photo is in the middle of the page, on the right side. The words at the bottom of the page are:

Tina Faelz was a quiet type, and a good friend to us. She always had a smile on her face, but basically kept to herself. Things were bright for her this year as she made many new friends. We'll miss her very much, and we're sorry it had to end this way.

Love always,
Her Friends

In Memory Of: Tina Faelz

Tina Faelz was a quiet type, and a good friend to us. She always had a smile on her face, but basically kept to herself. Things were bright for her this year as she made many new friends. We'll miss her very much, and we're sorry it had to end this way.
Love Always
Her Friends

The yearbook staff scrambled to place this full-page memorial of Tina Faelz in the yearbook. *From the Foothill High 1984 yearbook, courtesy of Kevin Wilson.*

The final line, "we're sorry it had to end this way," looks incredibly insensitive. None of Faelz's close friends recalled writing that paragraph or being involved with the wording. At best, it was a yearbook member, pressed for time, unsure or incapable of articulating the right words.

Drew Faelz at age ten, about three years after his sister's death. *Courtesy of Karin Reiff.*

DREW FAELZ'S LIFE WAS NEVER the same after his older sister's death. Over the next few years, he lived in fear of being the next victim, suffered from insomnia and called the police on multiple occasions after hearing noises in the backyard. Teachers and classmates who knew Drew as a quiet, friendly kid no longer knew how to act around him.

"I was always the kid whose sister got killed," Drew recalled. "I always felt whispers."

One day on the elementary school playground, an older classmate teased Drew that he killed Tina with a machete. His sister's murder followed him through grade school and, eventually, to his own freshman year at Foothill High. Six years later, there were reminders of her everywhere on campus, and her presence was overwhelming.

"I remember at times, I'd sit at lunch with my friends," Drew said. "We'd sit twenty feet from the memorial. Nobody ever brought it up to me, even at that point."

Eventually, Drew told his friends it was OK to discuss what happened. It brought him peace and helped him cope with her death. Still, Drew did not feel comfortable at Foothill High. He skipped class frequently, not because of partying but because he was working. Drew transferred to Village, a continuation high school, unaware it was the same path Steve Carlson took in 1985. Drew did not feel comfortable at that school either and ended up taking independent study to graduate.

As a young adult, Drew moved away from Pleasanton because home prices were too expensive, not because of what happened to his sister. In 1998, Drew and his wife had their first child. They named her Chloe Marie—the same middle name as his sister, Tina.

"I'm extremely proud of Drew of what he's accomplished in his young life," said his father, Steve Faelz. "He's got a good job. He's got interpersonal skills with human beings that I don't have. I don't know where he got that sense of humor around other people. The quick wit. I don't have that. I don't think his mom had that."

6
CREEPY GETS CREEPIER

That's probably the guy who killed Tina.
—*Weldon Mann*

FALL 1984-SUMMER 1987

Steve Carlson began his sophomore year at Foothill High in the fall of 1984. He was almost seventeen years old, drinking alcohol and smoking marijuana regularly, now dabbling in acid and crank and on the periphery of getting into trouble with the law. Carlson remained at Foothill long enough to get his sophomore year picture taken, which appeared in the yearbook, but did not finish the fall semester.

School records are sketchy because it was so long ago. Carlson was never a model student. But after the murder of Tina Faelz, he missed class regularly, his grades went down significantly and he was failing most classes.

"He became more visible to us after the stabbing," Foothill High assistant principal Jack Keegan said. "There were a number of times that I suspended him. He was drunk on campus. He was disruptive or high on drugs. I remember one time he was drunk on campus and yelling and flipping us off and saying, 'Eff you' across campus. We called the house and said, 'Your son is suspended again.'"

Carlson's next stop was Village High, a continuation high school for students with low grades, multiple absences or credit deficiencies. It was

Steve Carlson started his sophomore year at Foothill High and remained long enough to have this photo taken but transferred to Village Continuation School soon and later dropped out. *Courtesy of the Alameda County District Attorney's Office.*

established in 1978 as a "new beginning" for students who have not found success at either of the two comprehensive high schools in Pleasanton. It contained fewer students, lower teacher-to-student ratios and a focus on career interests and future goals.

His reputation as a troublemaker, and possibly being responsible for the death of Tina Faelz a year earlier, followed him to the new school. Carlson didn't seem to mind the attention.

Former classmate Aaron Rix noticed a dramatic difference in Carlson after Faelz's death. Previously, Carlson ran from other teens and frequently got beat up. Now that people whispered that Carlson was responsible for a murder, his peers were afraid of him. Carlson enjoyed his tough-guy reputation.

Rix estimated he hung out with Carlson twenty to thirty times in his life, before and after the murder. Rix said Carlson smoked some pot and mostly drank alcohol before the murder. Afterward, it became crank/speed, plus pot and alcohol.

"He became a meth head," Rix said. "He changed into a dirtier, creepier version that had this tag on him that he'd viciously stabbed this girl. Then from that point on, I remember the dude being spun out all the time."

Rob Tremblay knew Carlson from taking ceramics, wood shop and metal shop classes, plus mutual friends in the party scene. Tremblay recalled inappropriate comments from Carlson following the murder.

"He wasn't in mourning," Tremblay said. "I remember him discussing it and thinking, 'Shut up.' He was so openly joking about it. How could a person do that? He made jokes about it. He wanted attention, and that's what he got. He wanted to be that sick guy. I remember him saying, 'I think I'll go to 7-11 and say hello to Tina's mom.'"

KEITH CLOWARD LIVED A FEW BLOCKS over from Tina Faelz in the Valley Trails neighborhood. Cloward was a casual friend of Carlson. They had been classmates at Wells Middle School, briefly at Foothill High and again at Village High. They also were in juvenile hall together at the same time.

"I was a crazy motherfucker back then," Cloward admitted. "I was really nuts. We had competitions to see who could be sicker than [my friend] Phillip. Didn't matter if we got arrested or what."

One night, Cloward said, he and his friend got the idea to steal drugs from a known dealer who lived in a mobile home that he often parked at the Pleasanton Fairgrounds. They recruited Carlson, telling him it was a chance to "prove himself" and because the drug dealer didn't know Carlson.

According to Cloward, the plan was for Carlson to knock on the door, wearing a hoodie and point the gun at the dealer. Then the others would go inside and steal the drugs. They were worried about bringing an unloaded gun in case the dealer called their bluff and had a gun of his own. But they also didn't trust Carlson, so they only put two bullets in the gun.

The dealer and his mobile home weren't there. Upset that they weren't able to steal from him, the trio went on a rampage. Cloward said they destroyed anything they saw at the fairgrounds, breaking lights and other property, along with doing damage to the golf course.

They returned another night, trying the same plan, according to Cloward. This time, the drug dealer was home. Carlson pulled the gun and demanded the drugs, but the dealer wasn't intimidated. He confronted Carlson and grabbed him physically, and the three kids ran away before anybody was hurt or any guns were used.

Cloward and Carlson both spent time at the juvenile justice center in San Leandro. For those who knew Carlson was at juvenile hall, some thought he had been quietly arrested for Faelz's murder but the police couldn't release it publicly because he was a minor. That was not true.

Upon arrival, Cloward said the white kids were taught by fellow juvenile kids to memorize the lyrics to the Slayer song "Hell Awaits" as fast as possible. The reason? If you were scared by any of the black kids, you'd chant the words, and they'd leave you alone because the blacks were scared of crazy, satanic white boys.

The gates of hell lie waiting as you see
There's no price to pay, just follow me
I can take your lost soul from the grave
Jesus knows your soul cannot be saved

Crucify the so-called Lord; he soon shall fall to me
Your souls are damned; your God has fell
To slave for me eternally
Hell awaits

The juvenile hall kids weren't allowed to write letters to each other, yet Cloward said Carlson somehow figured out a way to write him three letters. Cloward doesn't remember the content of the letters. He does distinctly remember the names that Carlson signed on those letters: Charles Manson, Leonard Lake and Richard Ramirez (three of the most notorious killers in California history).

The weight room was a gathering place where Cloward saw Carlson most often. Cloward recalled that Carlson "could do pullups like a motherfucker" and transformed himself from a skinny guy with bony arms to a guy with fourteen-inch biceps.

"He was always fighting everybody," Cloward said. "If you said something, he's swinging. He'd hit you with these boney legs, but oh man, it hurt super bad. We're always hitting each other, trying to knock each other out when the counselors aren't looking. One day, I got my friend at the water fountain and gave him one of those knees. I dropped him. He couldn't believe it. My friend was twice as big as me. That move is devastating. That's what I learned from Carlson."

ASK PEOPLE THREE DECADES LATER, and they'll say Carlson was never invited to parties in the 1980s. He just showed up. That's possibly a convenient way of trying to distance themselves from admitting that they used to hang out with him. It's also a recurring sentiment heard over and over.

Many of the stories follow a familiar theme, like one told by Morgan Reece. It was a house party in the Pleasanton Meadows neighborhood in 1986 or 1987. Reece gave Carlson a ride to the party but isn't sure how or why, since they weren't close friends. Once at the party, Carlson was out of control.

"He was completely provocative," Reece said. "He was starting fights with everybody. It turned into a full-on brawl. We beat his ass down to the ground. He kept getting back up. He was completely maniacal. He would keep coming back for more. It went on and on. There was a lull, and we thought he would calm down. Then he would act up again and get beaten more. He was totally disjointed and a wreck. It was clear there was something wrong with him. The lights were just not on. It was a crazy night."

The crazy night ended with Reece still giving Carlson a ride home.

Unless they went to Village Continuation High, most teenagers in Pleasanton no longer had to deal with Carlson. But he was like the monster who suddenly reappeared at random locations. Weldon Mann, one of the last to see Tina Faelz alive, saw Carlson at an Oakland A's game.

"They had taken some of the juvy kids to an A's game," Mann said. "I was driving, so it was my junior or senior year. I thought Carlson was dead. I saw him in the detention stuff at the A's game. It was one of those random things, you bump into somebody, and then you realize that they're incarcerated. I think we actually discussed it on the way home, 'That's probably the guy who killed Tina.'"

The more Carlson drank and the more drugs he abused, the more his mouth became an issue. Stories abound that Carlson admitted at parties that he killed Tina Faelz and then said he was just kidding. Other times, he would make cryptic comments. Sometimes, people directly questioned or interrogated Carlson. Other times, he brought it up himself.

"He would always make little comments that were almost a direct confession," recalled Rix. "I remember him saying one time to us—it was so long ago, I'm off on the direct quote—but it was something like, 'Have you ever thought what it would be like to stab somebody? I know what it's like to push a knife in.'"

Rix recalled another occasion when Carlson showed up at his house for a party and was making similar comments.

"He came to the party and everybody was tripped out by it," Rix said. "What I remember the most was people saying, 'What the fuck is Steve doing here?' I didn't invite the dude. But I probably didn't invite 75 percent of the people at the party. I knew them, but people just showed up. I believe people were making comments to him. They were fucking with him. I wasn't there for the comments. I heard about it shortly later that Steve is telling some crazy ass shit, and people are going to kill him. We told Steve that he had to go."

Don Costa also heard one of these cryptic comments. Costa can't recall the exact date of this interaction. He thought it took place a few months after the murder, when he was smoking weed with Carlson and Darren Wilson at Carlson's house.

"I called him out," Costa said in a 2011 interview. "I said, 'Dude, did you kill her?' [He said,] 'Maybe I did, and maybe I didn't.' And that's when I saw the knife."

According to Costa, Carlson asked Wilson to get rid of the knife, and Wilson agreed. Costa continued:

I said, "No, you can't do that, you have to tell somebody about this."
That's when other people said, "You going to talk to the cops?" I might
have smoked weed back in the day. Like I told the cops, the only thing I had
to hide was whether I was smoking weed or if I had weed in my pocket. I
didn't care. I never lied about anything. These guys were not hunters. I'm a
hunter. To see that knife and to see blood on it, I was sure as the day is long
that he did it—because he was a fucking freak. I don't know, man. You
see that kind of look in somebody's eyes who does not care about people's
outlook and people's life, they will fucking kill you. And that's what I saw
in his eyes. He did not care. And he was in the right proximity and the
whole nine yards. To give me the answer that he did—"Maybe I did, and
maybe I didn't"—freaked me out.

(In 2011, Wilson agreed to an interview with this author to discuss this incident and other memories. He never showed up for the interview and stopped returning phone calls. When the district attorney's investigator interviewed Wilson in 2014, he denied Costa's story.)

The difficulty for the police in the 1980s, which became even more problematic in the 2010s, was the reliability of who actually heard Carlson confess and his or her intoxication level at the time.

The perfect example is a party at the house of Eric Becker around December 1985. Among those at the party were Steve Carlson, Joe LaPlante, Lonnie Brooks and Brooks's then-girlfriend Lisa Suchon (this author's older sister). However, no police report was ever filed.

In interviews for this book, Becker, Brooks and Suchon independently recalled Carlson was at the party and heard him confess to the murder. All three remembered that Suchon was freaked out by what she heard and immediately left the party with Brooks, intending to tell the police.

Sometime in January 1986, an anonymous person called Shirley Faelz and said he knew who killed her daughter. The distraught victim's mother called the police with details about the phone call. This is according to a March 1986 article in the *Oakland Tribune*.

Police were getting wind of these stories. It was time for detectives to start asking questions. They started with people who knew Carlson. Over a three-day stretch, from January 15 to 17, 1986, police interviewed Todd Smith, Lonnie Brooks, Joe LaPlante and Darren Wilson.

Twenty-one months prior, Smith's story had gone from providing Carlson an alibi to not knowing where his neighbor was when the murder took place. This time, Smith told police his memory was vague. Smith did not provide an alibi for Carlson. He also did not provide any information that Carlson was the killer.

Brooks actually told police he was at Carlson's house on the day of the murder and remembered him wearing a red flannel shirt. When asked why he remembered Carlson's red flannel shirt, Brooks told police he heard a psychic say the killer was wearing a red flannel shirt and that triggered his memory.

(In a 2015 interview, when told of his 1986 statement to police, Brooks insisted he was never at Carlson's house any day of his life, said he was riding horses near the crime scene with friends when he heard police sirens on the day of the murder and said he once slammed Carlson into a locker during a fight at summer school.)

Also in the 1986 report, Brooks stated he never heard a confession directly from Carlson. He said a group was discussing Carlson's possible involvement in the Faelz murder, giving their ideas and facts. Brooks told the police, "Talk to Joe LaPlante. He has all the facts."

LaPlante told detectives his brain was fried due to drugs but admitted he was the one who put Carlson in the garbage dumpster on the day of the murder. LaPlante said Carlson joked about killing Faelz because she wouldn't do his homework.

Wilson confirmed that Carlson had knives and told a similar story that Carlson joked about killing Faelz because she wouldn't do his homework.

On Thursday, January 16, 1986, Detectives Robert Fracoli and Gary Tollefson talked to Carlson from 3:28 p.m. until 5:30 p.m. Carlson was in juvenile hall at the time. Fracoli read Carlson his Miranda rights. Carlson declined to have his parents present at the questioning and signed the admonition and waiver form.

On Friday, January 17, 1986, Tollefson and Fracoli talked to Carlson again. This time, it was from 1:05 p.m. to 3:05 p.m. As was standard practice at the time, Carlson was offered a cigarette. He accepted it.

Over the course of two days, Carlson told the detectives he couldn't remember everything clearly from the day of the murder, and he had been using drugs for quite a few years. Carlson did remember driving his mother's car (a Mercury Montego) and that Todd Smith was riding in it. Carlson also remembered riding a moped around the neighborhood with Smith and seeing Faelz coming through a hole in the fence as she walked home.

Carlson also told the detectives he watched the police at the crime scene from the roof of his house on the day of the murder, which matches Tollefson's report from April 5, 1984.

When asked if he had any social interaction with Faelz, Carlson said no. At most, Carlson told detectives, he walked past her in the hallway and said hello. Carlson admitted that he joked about killing Faelz because she wouldn't do his homework but did not really do it. Carlson admitted to having a pocketknife but had given it away in 1985.

Tollefson said, "He didn't seem terribly concerned that he was being accused of murder and was laughing like he was joking with us."

"I'd say that he was a bit anxious or nervous, but he was cooperative. He was pretty flat as far as he didn't vary in his emotions too much through the interview," Fracoli said.

Tollefson and Fracoli were suspicious of Carlson. It didn't make sense for somebody to brag about a murder he did not commit. But they didn't arrest him. Carlson remained in juvenile hall. A drugged-out kid bragging at parties and a bunch of stoned teenagers sitting around sharing stories wasn't enough to arrest somebody. There was no real evidence. It would never hold up in court.

On January 16, 1986, the same day that Fracoli and Tollefson spoke to Carlson, Detective Robert Lyness obtained the purse of Tina Faelz out of evidence. This was the first time the purse had been touched since April 1984. Lyness was directed to look for latent fingerprints. Lyness visually examined the purse. He did not notice any bloodstains. He performed "superglue fuming" of the purse. No identifiable prints were found. Lyness returned the purse to evidence.

On January 20, 1986, Lyness submitted the purse to the FBI for additional latent print development using technology that was not available to the Pleasanton Police Department. Lyness wrote a cover letter outlining the request.

On February 16, 1986, the purse was returned to Lyness from the FBI. No prints were found.

On February 18, 1986, the purse was returned to the evidence room. Nobody touched the purse for another twenty-two years.

In the March 24, 1986 edition of the *Oakland Tribune*, then-Lieutenant Mike Stewart told reporter Benny Evangelista, "We had high hopes that we could fall into the rumor mill and get something. After extensive man hours, we determined it was a bunch of dopers mouthing off."

IN 1988, FOUR YEARS AFTER the murder, Todd Smith applied for a job with the city of Pleasanton as a community service officer (CSO). His ultimate goal was to become a police officer. He thought this would be a good start.

Considering his previous questioning in the Faelz case, police performed an extensive background check and talked to Smith's neighbors and his boss at Marina Plumbing.

Smith took a psych exam. He was asked to take a lie detector test, which he thought would be centered on the potential job. Instead, Smith was peppered with questions about the murder of Faelz.

This time, Smith included some statements that he thought Steve Carlson was responsible for the murder. In the span of four years, Smith had gone from providing an alibi for Carlson to having a vague memory about everything to suggesting it was Carlson. The police didn't know what to believe...

Smith did not get the CSO job. His employer was scared off from the line of questioning and fired him from his plumbing job. Smith's father, the chief building inspector in Pleasanton, contacted a lawyer.

"We were going to get an attorney and sue," Smith said. "They said it was a million dollars, easy. They can't do that. But my dad was worried about losing his job. So we didn't pursue it any further."

Todd Smith was furious with the Pleasanton Police Department. Resentful and angry, Smith never said another word to authorities about the case for twenty-five years.

WHEN NOT IN JUVENILE HALL, Steve Carlson was usually still living with his family on Lemonwood Way in Pleasanton. The neighborhood had changed. The other side of Lemonwood had new homes, and the murder scene was now somebody's backyard.

The entrance to the Creek was gone because of a sound wall that was added to minimize the noise entering the neighborhood from Interstate 680, and a fence prevented kids from walking to the highway.

Carlson's elder sister Tanya had moved out. His younger siblings Richie and Amy, the twins, felt the impact more than anybody else of living with a drug-addicted, erratic elder brother with an unsavory reputation and a bad habit of joking about a murder that happened across the street.

Richie was confronted at school multiple times by kids who accused his brother of the murder. According to people who witnessed these confrontations, sometimes Richie would defend his brother. Sometimes he would try to distance himself from his brother.

"It was sad," said Brandie Provost, who had once used her backpack to prevent Steve from raping her older sister. "I didn't think Steve was necessarily always nice to Amy and Richie. From what I could tell, he wasn't around a whole lot. Maybe it's because he was running in circles and getting

This is where Ashwood Drive becomes Lemonwood Way in the Muirwood Meadows neighborhood. The Carlson house is on the left corner. The crime scene was built over a few years later and is now somebody's backyard. *Photo by the author.*

Opposite, top: A chain-link fence prevents people from going into the small area separating houses on Lemonwood Drive and Ashton Lane, which leads to Interstate 680. *Photo by the author.*

into trouble. Richie and Amy didn't really talk. They had to have heard the rumors. How could they not? They didn't necessarily say anything about it or try to say no."

Provost believes that the rumors of Steve killing Tina Faelz—and his ongoing behavior—had a major negative impact on the twins.

"After this whole thing happened, it did change them," Provost said. "Amy had her issues. Richie had his issues...It was kinda like the innocence of everything just crumbled. I often wondered, 'Did they know anything? Were they afraid to say anything? Were they afraid of him?' As long as I can remember, every single person, the first name that came off their tongue was Steve Carlson."

Steve and Richie Carlson fought like any set brothers, yet the words that accompanied those fights were different than the standard brotherly fight.

The only indication of where kids would enter the Creek area is this fenced-off area where Lemonwood meets Ashton. *Photo by the author.*

"Richie used to call [Steve] on it," said Art Guzman, a close childhood friend of Richie. "He would say, 'You know you did it, you piece of shit.' They would start arguing. Steve would say, 'Yeah, I did' and then later he would recant. Richie would push him on it. It wasn't brotherly love. They weren't best buds. They do have their bond. They are brothers. They got in trouble together. Richie resents his brother a lot. Steve was nothing but a negative influence on him."

At various times, Carlson was either kicked out of his home or avoiding his parents. He stole checks from his parents that he tried to cash and also stole Richie's coin collection. He ended up bouncing around houses of various neighbors between 1985 and '87.

Guzman convinced his parents to let Carlson stay at their house briefly. One day, Guzman answered the door, and it was the police. Guzman was asked if the family owned a gun. Guzman said yes, his father was a cop and had a .22 pistol. When he went to retrieve the gun, he realized it was gone.

"I didn't know it, but Steve stole my dad's .22 pistol," Guzman said. "He was getting chased by the cops for some reason, and he ditched it. He threw the gun. The cops recovered it. The serial number was registered to my dad. Right after that, he was just gone. I've never seen him again."

Andrew Hartlett, who cut school briefly on the day of the murder to hang out with Carlson and two others, saw Carlson at the park in the Val Vista housing tract occasionally. They hung out in Sunol one day. On another more memorable day, Hartlett returned home with his girlfriend and suspected a stranger was inside his house.

"[Carlson] was hiding in the closet," Hartlett said. "I told him to get the fuck out. I didn't see him for weeks. Then one day, my dad caught him sleeping on the couch. When my dad got a piece of him, he told him to stick it and never come back. That was the last time I saw him."

As of November 4, 1986, Carlson was still in the San Francisco Bay Area because he was cited in Walnut Creek for failure to stop at a stop sign and no proof of car registration. By the 1987–88 school year, this author was a freshman at Foothill High, and the Carlson twins were juniors.

Amy ran away from home a couple times. The first time was after she was caught smoking and drinking with her friends. Amy's punishment was indefinite restriction at home, so she decided to run away. Amy got on a bus bound for Bakersfield that departed from the Livermore bus depot. She ended up in Stockton on a stopover. Amy's plan was to sleep in a tree until the next bus came. Before the next bus arrived, her parents found her. One of Amy's friends had tipped off her parents. It was an agonizing decision.

The open quad section of Foothill High's campus in the late 1980s. *From the author's collection.*

The friend felt bad for snitching on Amy but was genuinely concerned Amy would get hurt.

The second time Amy ran away, it was for multiple weeks. Tanya said her parents filed a missing-persons report. Even Amy's closest friends didn't know her whereabouts this time.

"I wouldn't see her for a long time and [was] not sure what was going on with her," Guzman said. "Then I'm sitting at home one day, and I hear somebody knock on the door, and it's Amy. She looked totally different. Her hair was dyed black and all short. Same old Amy, though, laughing and giggling. It was like, 'Wow, where have you been?'"

Amy only told a few close friends and her parents why she ran away: because her elder brother Steve had molested her. Reactions were mixed. Steve was such a troublemaker—you could tell any story about him, and it was believable. However, Amy was known for telling lies, too. Would Steve really molest his younger sister? Would Amy really make up that lie about her brother?

Amy has also told close friends that a cousin molested her as well. Amy didn't think her parents believed her claim about Steve. The turbulent relationship with her parents continued to deteriorate. It would be over twenty years before Amy tried to repair things with her mother.

Richie Carlson struggled with his own addictions to drugs and alcohol as a teenager and into his twenties. Richie went to rehab, got clean and remains sober to this day.

How much was Steve Carlson to blame for the twins' downward spiral? It's hard to say definitively, though clearly it was a factor.

Steve Carlson had completely worn out his welcome in Pleasanton. He was a high-school dropout, hooked on drugs, recently out of juvenile hall, suspected of murder by neighbors, wasn't welcome anywhere in town, molested his own sister and his immediate family wanted nothing to do with him.

One of the few people willing to give him a chance was a grandmother in Davis.

7
AN UNUSUAL TASK FORCE

We're still with no leads and no place to go on it right now.
—Mike Stewart

MARCH 24, 1986-JANUARY 2009

Too many teenage girls were missing. Too many teenage girls were dead. There were too many from the same area. And none of the crimes were solved. It had been almost two years since Tina Faelz was stabbed to death in broad daylight as she walked home from school. The headline in the March 24, 1986 edition of the *Oakland Tribune* was "Slain Women's Families Cope with Strain of Unsolved Cases."

In 1986, an unusual task force was created, combining the efforts of police and sheriff's department detectives across Alameda County and Contra Costa County to study four similar cases:

- On December 2, 1983, fourteen-year-old Kellie Jean Poppelton was found fatally beaten, stabbed and suffocated in a wooded area off Kilkare Road in a small, unincorporated area between Fremont and Pleasanton called Sunol.
- On April 5, 1984, fourteen-year-old Tina Faelz was stabbed forty-four times on her way home from school in Pleasanton.

Unsolved murders of 5 girls haunt Eastbay citizens, police

SUN JUL 15 1984 EB

"I really need to see the person caught who did this. Not just for our sake, but for the whole community, because there's still a lot of fear out there."
— Arthur Costas, father of Orinda slaying victim

"If this case doesn't get solved it won't be for lack of effort."
— Lt. James Robinson of Contra Costa County

By Jack Cheevers and Harry Harris
The Tribune

The climate of fear of which Arthur Costas speaks and Lt. Robinson's investigative efforts extend far beyond the rolling hills of Orinda.

Families and detectives in both Contra Costa and Alameda counties share the trauma and pressure caused by murders of five girls slain since last November.

The dead are:

■ Angela Bugay, 5, the Antioch girl who vanished from in front of her apartment building on Nov. 19, 1983. Her body was found a week later, buried in a field about three miles from her home.

■ Kirsten Costas, 15, a popular Miramonte High School student who was stabbed repeatedly on a neighbor's porch after being lured to what she thought was a sorority initiation.

■ Kellie Jean Poppleton, 14, of Fremont, who was found fatally beaten, stabbed and suffocated Dec. 2 in a wooded area off Kilkare Road near Sunol.

■ Tina Marie Faelz, 14, of Pleasanton, who was found dead of more than 15 stab wounds April 5 in a freeway culvert near her school.

On Friday, Pleasanton Chief of Police Bill Eastman said one individual — not one of classmate Tina's classmates — is the target of their investigation.

■ Julie A. Connell, 18, of San Leandro, who was found slashed to death in Palomares Canyon outside Castro Valley on April 25, five days after she vanished from a Hayward Park.

No one has been charged in any of the cases, although task forces have been formed, uncounted hours spent in investigation, hundreds of witnesses and possible suspects inter-

See MURDERS, Page A-9

From the July 15, 1984 edition of the *Oakland Tribune*. Police from different agencies formed an unusual task force to see if similar crimes against teenage girls were related. *From the author's collection.*

Faelz was killed about ten miles from where Poppelton's body was discovered.

- On April 25, 1984, eighteen-year-old Julie A. Connell was found slashed to death in Palomares Canyon outside Castro Valley. She had vanished from a park in Hayward five days earlier. It was three weeks after Faelz's death.

- On November 28, 1984, eighteen-year-old Lisa Monzo was reported missing in Hayward. She was last seen alive walking through the rain near the Nimitz Freeway (Interstate 580). Four days later, her strangled body was discovered.

104

Poppelton's case was the most vexing because of the strange twists and turns. A thirteen-year-old girl confessed to the murder and implicated three others. But she later admitted to fabricating the entire story. Fremont police wasted weeks of valuable time chasing an elaborate hoax and never found the real killer.

If authorities were skeptical of listening to teenagers in Pleasanton gossip that a neighborhood teenager was responsible for Faelz's death, perhaps the Poppelton case was a reason. The Alameda Sheriff's Department and Fremont police were embarrassed for botching the investigation and prematurely arresting three innocent individuals.

Ultimately, the task force came to an end with a few suspects but no concrete evidence and no arrests. Other than their ages, there were no apparent connections between the girls.

"It's extremely frustrating," Pleasanton police lieutenant Mike Stewart, head of the unit investigating Faelz's death, told the *Oakland Tribune*. "We're still with no leads and no place to go on it right now. We still have a chance. But every day that goes by, there's less [of a chance]."

ON JANUARY 30, 1989, THIRTEEN-YEAR-OLD Ilene Misheloff was last seen walking from Wells Middle School in Dublin to her ice skating coach's home on Alegre Drive. Misheloff never made it. She took a popular shortcut for teenagers, a ditch that runs along the edge of Mape Park, which was eerily reminiscent of what Faelz did.

One of the last places Misheloff was seen walking was past the Foster's Freeze in Dublin. That restaurant was owned by Tanya Carlson's then-boyfriend and now-husband Walt Pittson. Amy and Richie Carlson worked at the restaurant, but Steve Carlson never did.

Robert Misheloff, Ilene's elder brother, worked at the Foster's Freeze, too. Missing fliers of Ilene were plastered over the restaurant's walls. Her disappearance touched the Pittson family deeply.

On the anniversary of Misheloff's disappearance every year, her family holds a candlelight walk on the route she took that day. Tanya and her family have made that walk, along with hundreds more. Tanya has spoken numerous times with Ilene's parents, Mike and Maddi Misheloff, at an office where they continue to headquarter the search for their daughter.

For Wells Middle School, it was the third girl in eight years who had walked those hallways and was now in the newspaper headlines for all the wrong reasons. Kellie Poppelton. Tina Faelz. And now Ilene Misheloff.

THE FAMILY OF LISA ANN MONZO was the first to get answers about what happened to their daughter. Alameda County senior deputy district attorney Rockne Harmon built a revolutionary case, using a fairly new technology called DNA, in Alameda County Superior Court in Oakland against a man named Michael Ihde.

On November 6, 1996, a jury found Ihde guilty of the rape and murder of Monzo. Ihde was already serving a life sentence in Washington State for the death of another woman.

In the years leading up to the trial, Pleasanton police looked for clues linking Ihde to Faelz. They received phone calls from residents who provided phone numbers of people who knew Ihde. They learned that Ihde lived in Pleasanton on Alvarado Street from June 1983 until late 1984 or early 1985. The most chilling was a photo that Shirley Faelz produced of Shirley, Drew and a man who sure looked like Ihde.

"Shirley brought that photo in to me," Tollefson said. "She thought that was Ihde, and we'd already been looking at Ihde and we thought, 'Oh my goodness, it is Ihde!'"

Drew Faelz was working at the Fresh Choice at the Stoneridge Mall in Pleasanton. It was a few years after he'd graduated from high school. The police showed him the photo one day at work.

Investigators went to Spokane, Washington, to interview two friends of Shirley who had introduced her to the guy in the photograph. In separate interviews, they identified the male as a friend who had been in their wedding party. It was not Michael Ihde.

"It was a true look-alike," Tollefson said.

AS THE 1990s CONTINUED, science became more sophisticated and helped solve other cold cases, and the Pleasanton police hoped that science would give them a lead on the Faelz case, too.

In 1994, Steve Hayes was the director of the Alameda County Sheriff's Office Crime Lab. Pleasanton police submitted a request for latent print analysis of a matchbook, two schoolbooks, a blue binder and papers that belonged to Tina Faelz.

No prints were found on *Preparing to Use Algebra*. Some small prints were found on *Flowers in the Attic*—and those belonged to Faelz. Presumptive blood was found on the books and binder.

Still, it did not yield any suspects.

ON DECEMBER 2, 1997, TWENTY-TWO-YEAR-OLD Vanessa Lei Samson was kidnapped as she walked to work on West Las Positas Drive in Pleasanton. It was less than half a mile from where Tina Faelz was killed. Samson's body was found, two days later, in Lake Tahoe. It was partially frozen, and she had a ligature mark around her neck. It would later be learned that James Daveggio and Michelle Michaud were responsible for her abduction, rape and murder.

Daveggio's background caught the attention of Pleasanton police in a dramatic way. He'd attended Foothill High in 1977 after transferring from James Logan High in Union City. At various times, Daveggio lived with his parents in Pleasanton on Clovewood Lane, which was twelve blocks from Lemonwood Way and the murder scene. The backyard of the Daveggios' house backed up against the Creek.

Surely, Daveggio knew about the shortcut under Interstate 680 and had explored the Creek like other teenagers in the area. The Creek, in fact, goes all the way into Sunol, where Poppelton was found dead.

Was it possible Daveggio committed the murder of Faelz and used the Creek to get home, rather than traversing through the streets, where he might get spotted with bloody clothes?

Daveggio had reconciled with his ex-wife in March 1984 and lived with her in Livermore until May 1984. His ex-wife told police that Daveggio drank excessively, used crank, gambled heavily and would disappear for one to two days at a time with no explanation. His ex-wife also said she didn't recall him acting suspiciously, changing his appearance or telling her that he ever hurt somebody.

In July 1984, three months after the death of Faelz, Pleasanton police took Daveggio into custody for a different offense. He was charged with kidnapping and forced oral copulation on a woman he met at the bar inside Black Angus on Hopyard Road. Luck was on Daveggio's side in that case. The charges were dropped due to lack of evidence and unreliable testimony of the victim, who was drunk and only had a vague recollection.

The 1997 lead on Daveggio, based on the Vanessa Sansom murder, did not lead to any additional clues about the Faelz murder.

PLEASANTON POLICE CONTINUED HOPING that improved science would give them a lead on the Tina Faelz case. In 2001, criminologist and forensic scientist Alan Keel examined evidence in the case. He tested the dried material on the victim's abdomen, a bloody stain from her clothing and fingernail clippings for any foreign DNA. All the DNA discovered matched Faelz.

In February 2003, more testing was done on the dry material on Faelz's abdomen. In August 2003, more testing was done on Faelz's fingernail clippings. Again, no foreign DNA was discovered.

In 2007, THE FAMILY OF JULIE CONNELL became the next to get answers on what happened to their daughter. A jury convicted Robert Rhoades, formerly of San Lorenzo, of tying up, raping and slashing the throat of Connell. Rhoades was already on death row for the 1996 kidnap, torture and murder of eight-year-old Michael Lyons of Yuba City (about forty-five miles north of Sacramento).

The arrest and subsequent conviction of Rhoades led investigators throughout the Bay Area to reopen their files to see if Rhoades could be linked to their long-unsolved murders.

Once again, the Pleasanton police looked for clues linking Rhoades with the death of Faelz. But no evidence existed to connect Rhoades with her murder.

In DECEMBER 2002, JAMES DAVEGGIO was interviewed at San Quentin Prison, this time by Dublin police about the Misheloff case. In January 2003, Daveggio was interviewed again, this time by Pleasanton detective Darrin Davis.

Daveggio told investigators he was a good friend of Walter Nyman, the Pleasanton man responsible for the attempted rape of a girl just outside Santa Cruz five days after the Faelz murder. Daveggio stated he was not involved in the Misheloff or Faelz cases, but he believed Nyman could be responsible for either, plus the Kellie Poppelton death. Daveggio said Nyman was a "much more aggressive sexual assaulter" than he was.

Daveggio added that if he'd had something to do with the Misheloff disappearance, he would tell them, because he wanted to bring closure to the family, and he had nothing to lose serving a life sentence. Police remained very suspicious of Nyman. But they still had no firm evidence.

In October 2008, Daveggio's name reappeared yet again. Pleasanton police received a tip from a former law enforcement source who heard from a source that Daveggio told a former cellmate he killed a girl, "cut her real bad" and left her body in a ditch. It wasn't clear if the tip was related to the Samson case, Misheloff case, Faelz case or Poppelton case.

When questioned directly, the former cellmate denied he ever heard Daveggio state those things. When pressed, the former cellmate said he was talking about the Faelz and Misheloff cases at Pastime Pool Hall with friends, and they commented that Daveggio "probably" had something to do with it. Pleasanton police thought the cellmate was being evasive and might know more, but the tip stalled.

To this day, the Kellie Poppelton murder remains unsolved. The decision to cremate her body, so she could rest with her maternal grandmother, has unwittingly prevented modern-day DNA from being able to identify her killer.

To this day, the Ilene Misheloff disappearance remains unsolved as well.

8
FROM PLEASANTON TO DAVIS

I never saw a case of alcoholism as severe as him.
—*Jon Adler*

1987-2010

Tina Faelz would have graduated from Foothill High in 1987. Her death was remembered with a moment of silence at the graduation ceremonies at the Pleasanton Fairgrounds. Steve Carlson wasn't there. He had dropped out years before, never coming close to the credits required to graduate.

Carlson moved to Davis to live with his grandmother. She gave him a place to stay and an opportunity at a fresh start and hoped she could help him get straightened out. Nobody knew him in Davis. Nobody called him creepy. Nobody suspected he might be responsible for the death of Tina Faelz. He was a good-looking guy, tall and lean, with bright blue eyes and a thick mop of blond hair.

It was in 1988 when twenty-year-old Steve Carlson met a senior at King High named Justine Hamilton. She was born in Alaska to a teenage mother who likely used speed and drank alcohol during her pregnancy. Justine was adopted by a couple who both worked in education.

"When I first met him, it was clear that he wasn't who I wanted her around," said Justine's adoptive mother, Janet. "He wasn't employed. He didn't seem to have any family. He didn't have an address. But I hadn't seen what he was capable of, at that point. He was actually very charming."

Janet recalled that Carlson usually wore T-shirts or flannel shirts. He'd wear jeans or cutoff jeans as shorts. He was almost always clean-shaven. His blond hair was usually hidden under a baseball cap.

As she matured in her teens, Justine Hamilton progressed from a passive kid in grade school to a rebel who had a habit of getting involved with sketchy people and being very loyal to them. Still, even her closest friends wondered what she saw in Carlson.

"Steve paid attention to her," explained Rachel Silva, a close friend of hers from grade school. "That's what she was seeking. I didn't know their relationship. I don't know if it was abusive or happy. I don't know if they were happy. It couldn't be healthy. They were using IV drugs. I know the group of people they were hanging out with were criminals. They weren't good people. I was going on a totally different path in my life and just decided not to have them in my life."

Another one of Justine's closest friends was Tracy Barton. Her ex-husband, Jon Adler, said none of Justine's friends liked Carlson. "We tolerated him because of Justine," Adler said. "If Justine had not been there, he wouldn't have been near us. Everybody loved Justine. She was a fun girl to be around. Very likeable. So you tolerated Steve's drunken antics."

Adler admits their crew was not a group of choirboys. They were teenagers who drank and smoked pot on most weekend nights. But the level of drinking for Carlson was beyond his comprehension.

"He was a late-stage alcoholic very early on," said Adler, sober since 1995 and now a counselor. "I never saw a case of alcoholism as severe as him. He could look pretty fucking pathetic the day after. You almost felt sorry for him. He'd try to portray that tough guy, and he'd start peeing on himself. The word pathetic came up a lot. You'd shake your head and say, 'Dude, really?' Something was going on inside him. Some kind of demon—twenty-two-year-old kids don't get drunk and pee on themselves."

One night, late in the summer of 1989, changed Steve Carlson's life and started a chain reaction that would lead to multiple trips to jail. Carlson was hanging out with a group of young teenagers near the University Mall. Carlson bought them alcohol. As the night continued, the group broke up and headed home, based on the various curfews their parents set. The final three people left were Carlson and two thirteen-year-old girls.

"He bought us more alcohol," said Jessica Hart, one of those two girls remaining. "He had his pit bull dog. I was getting freaked out by him. At first, he was showing interest in me. I was less under the influence than my friend. I was blowing him off. I was more interested in the dog. Somehow, we walked across the street to the UC [University of California] dorms. I was sitting in the parking lot on the curb. I was basically holding the dog."

Hart's friend went behind the dorms with Carlson. A few moments later, Hart heard her friend screaming and sprinted around the corner to their location.

"What I remember seeing is he was on top of her," Hart said. "And she was screaming, 'Get off me!' I was running over there and yelled, 'What are you doing? She's only thirteen! You're twenty-two!' It was just awful. At some point, he gets up and talks to me. He's gesturing to me about how it wouldn't go in. And then something about, 'I wanted you.'"

According to Hart, she ran across the street to call her mom from a pay phone, and Carlson took off. Hart's mother picked up the two teenage girls and learned what happened on the drive home. The victim's parents went to UC Davis police to file charges. A few days later, Hart identified Carlson in a police lineup.

At the time, Carlson was still seeing Justine Hamilton, and her mother, Janet, worked for UC Davis.

"I just remember the lieutenant who talked to me about it later, saying that when they arrested him, he still had her scarf," Janet Hamilton said. "He acted like it was the beginning of a beautiful relationship."

Carlson was charged with lewd and lascivious acts on a child. He was sentenced to three years in the California State Prison in Vacaville and was housed from May 29, 1990, to April 29, 1992.

(In a 2015 letter from prison, Carlson disputed the charges and referred to the details contained in the police report. According to a spokeswoman with the UC Davis police department, Case #8909-0383 met the criteria to get purged because of how long ago it happened. Even if the report did still exist, it was protected because of the victim's age.)

Despite the problems they were having, despite the lewd and lascivious acts on a thirteen-year-old girl and despite getting sent to jail, Justine Hamilton wasn't ready to give up on Steve Carlson. Justine didn't have a car. But she convinced her father, her mother, her friends and her friends' boyfriends to give her rides to see Carlson in prison.

"She was desperate to see him," Janet said. "I took her down to Vacaville to visit him quite a few times. She didn't think she could live without him. There's no question in my mind that she was in love with him."

Once she turned twenty-one, Justine Hamilton married Steve Carlson during a prison visit. This is how Janet Hamilton found out about her daughter's wedding: "He had his W2 forms sent to one of Justine's friends' parents. This was really embarrassing for me. The mom worked for me on campus. She called to tell me my son-in-law's W2 form is there. I said, 'I don't have a son-in-law.'"

But now, she did.

Most of Justine's friends didn't know why Carlson was in prison. Once Carlson was released, he usually told people it was due to drugs or burglary or

Steve Carlson with wife Justine shortly after the birth of their daughter. *Courtesy of Janet Hamilton.*

assault. But the town of Davis is small, and the real story of his incarceration began to spread. Carlson became a target of guys looking to deliver their own brand of vigilante justice.

"For as big of a guy as he was, he got beat up a lot," Adler said. "It wasn't that he started fights. He would just piss people off and not be in any shape to fight. That was his biggest weakness. Every time he fought, he was too shitfaced to defend himself."

Steve Carlson became a father about the same time his elder and younger sisters also had children. When sober and present, Steve was a loving and proud father. *Courtesy of Janet Hamilton.*

Carlson was required to register as a sex offender. About six months after he was released, in October 1992, Justine became pregnant. Previously, Justine had had two abortions. She kept the child this time. Steve and Justine's daughter was born on June 15, 1993. (For privacy, her name is not being used.)

Both of Carlson's sisters had babies around the same time. The family got together at an aunt's house and took pictures.

"He looked really good," his elder sister Tanya said. "He was so excited to be a dad. He just loved that baby. I really thought he was going to get it all together."

That was one of the last times Carlson saw anybody from his family. He was around a couple times for Christmas. But the visits became less and less frequent, often because Carlson was back in jail. Tanya saw her brother around 1993 and wouldn't see him again for another eighteen years.

On July 10, 1993, Justine's best friend from childhood, Rachel Silva, married her high school sweetheart, Mike Towle. Justine was a bridesmaid. Carlson met her at the wedding. "Steve came up to me and said that he wanted to give that to Justine—a big wedding," Towle said. "He was kinda crying. He was really drunk, saying, 'I just want this for Justine.'"

As the night progressed, Carlson's boozing continued, and his inebriated antics became more uncomfortable. The bride's stepfather, who worked in law enforcement, had to defuse the situation.

"Justine was getting embarrassed by his behavior," Towle said. "She told him several times to calm down. They were making a scene. It wasn't her. It was him. They left. It was tough because Justine didn't want to leave. She was in tears. But he wouldn't leave without her. He apologized. He said he wasn't trying to ruin our wedding. I guess it brought up feelings of a life that he wanted but didn't quite have."

Being married to Steve Carlson was not always miserable. Justine would often admit to her friends that Steve could be an asshole, but they never saw his sweet, sensitive side. Justine was always loyal. And initially, Carlson showed legitimate intentions of being a responsible father.

"When I was there, he was pretty good with [his daughter]," Janet said. "He'd play with her and hold her. He seemed very proud of her. He was pretty careful around me about his behavior when he was sober. When he was drunk, he couldn't help himself."

The couple moved from one apartment to the next, always leaving a wreck behind. The dog would poop on the carpet. The apartments had the

Steve Carlson attends to his daughter and a friend's daughter while Richie looks on at Steve's daughter's first birthday party in 1994. *Courtesy of Janet Hamilton.*

repugnant odor of drug use. They were evicted once for the condition of the apartment.

"I gave her an allowance because I didn't want that child on the street," Janet said. "I saw some of the physical damage he did to the apartments that I had to pay to rebuild. I know Justine used to call the police on him. Sometimes, she'd call me because she was embarrassed to call the cops again. I'd go over and throw him out."

The daughter's first birthday was June 15, 1994. A festive birthday party was held, with most of Justine's family attending. Carlson was fairly well behaved. He even brought his younger brother, Richie Carlson, to the party. It was the first—and only—time that the Hamiltons met any member of Steve's family.

"The nicest day we had was that first birthday, which is why I remember it so well," Janet said. "I remember it so well because he brings Richie. I think

The only time Janet Hamilton met anybody from Steve Carlson's family was when his younger brother Richie (on the right) came to the first birthday party of Steve and Justine's daughter. *Courtesy of Janet Hamilton.*

it's wonderful because he's reconnecting with his family. Maybe there will be a good influence."

But Carlson's drug and alcohol use ensured the good times didn't last long. Justine's relationship with Carlson caused a lot of her friends to keep their distance or sever their friendships entirely, including close childhood friend Tracy Barton.

"The memories I have of Steve Carlson are all bad," Barton said. "Steve beat Justine and wrecked her vehicles. I stopped hanging out with Justine for a few years because of him. He broke into my apartment and stole from me. He is not a good person. I always knew that he gave me a bad vibe."

Barton's ex-husband, Jon Adler, usually answered the door when Justine came to their house after Carlson physically abused her. He lost count how many times it occurred. The scenarios were similar. Justine would come inside the house, crying and in pain. Her friends would help. Her friends would ask if she was going to leave Carlson. She would say absolutely. Her friends would ask if she was going to the police. She would say, "Absolutely."

Then, hours later, she would return to the home where Carlson had just beaten her.

One of the hardest days of Adler's life, he said, was when a bloody Justine knocked on the door after another beating. "There was genuine concern for the way he treated her," Adler said. "Finally, I said, 'I can't do this. It hurts too bad. I love you. Every time I open the door, you go back to him. I'm causing my own pain.' I shut the door. It was way too painful to sit there and watch that. She would keep going back to him."

Being a father didn't change Steve Carlson. But being a mother finally changed Justine Hamilton's tolerance for her husband's behavior.

"Once Steve started to get into trouble with [their daughter] around, Justine started having doubts," Janet said. "It's not something she willingly shared with me. She did admit to me that she is the one who called his parole officer and got him violated, and sent back where he was, when she filed for divorce. We had to track him down. I had a friend who was an ex-cop who had a PI license. He served him."

The divorce was completed in 1996. Even after the divorce, Carlson wasn't totally out of the Hamiltons' lives. The police showed up at Justine's house looking for Carlson.

"They wouldn't believe her when she said she didn't know where he was," Janet said. "I remember being stopped at Safeway [and told] that my son-in-law was stealing from the store, and I needed to do something about it because he was going to get arrested. I said, 'Arrest his ass. He's not my son-in-law anymore.'"

ON AUGUST 22, 1996, John and Sandra Carlson sold their house on Lemonwood Way in Pleasanton for $285,000 and moved to Gardnerville, Nevada.

Steve Carlson was estranged from his parents and siblings. They weren't aware of his arrest for the incident in Davis. Tanya said she found out because a friend's husband was a police officer. Seemingly out of the blue, but not really, the friend suggested they go on the Megan's Law website to look at various names.

"That's how I found out," Tanya said. "We were shocked. Just shocked."

Two decades later, Steve told his sister Tanya that the incident ruined how he felt about himself and all he wanted to do was die. Steve contracted hepatitis C from his drug use. He figured he was going to die soon anyway, so he didn't register as a sex offender and, essentially, was trying to drink himself to death.

His plans for an alcohol-fueled suicide were thwarted by return trips to jail, where he'd get clean and sober and receive medical treatment.

SARAH WHITMIRE WAS SEVENTEEN years old and living on the couch of a cockroach-infested apartment in Davis with a man named Aaron. He was much older and had a bad drug problem, but Aaron had a charitable heart and was there to help somebody in need. Whitmire was in need.

Her mother was an alcoholic and a mean one. She moved in with her dad at age fourteen. A year later, she was homeless, living on the streets or house hopping. Whitmire was given a warm place to live on Aaron's couch.

It just so happened that Aaron's apartment was across the street from where Steve Carlson, Justine Hamilton and their daughter lived. Whitmire heard the couple fighting a lot. Hamilton routinely locked Carlson out of the house, so he'd go to Aaron's apartment across the street.

Whitmire's initial impression was that Carlson was a loser. Her father already knew Carlson, having played in poker games with him when Whitmire was much younger. Whitmire's father once said his worst nightmare was his daughter ever dating "Psycho" Steve Carlson.

Carlson tried getting Hamilton and Whitmire to become friends. Hamilton offered to do Whitmire's hair one day and made her a grilled cheese sandwich another day. Whitmire played with the couple's daughter. Hamilton never warmed up to Whitmire, though. She was resentful of the younger, thinner Whitmire. Carlson didn't immediately express any romantic interest in Whitmire.

That all changed, probably not by coincidence, once Whitmire turned eighteen. Carlson wasn't about to touch a girl under eighteen again, not after spending three years in jail for what he thought was a consensual encounter. Once Whitmire turned eighteen, Carlson essentially moved into Aaron's apartment and became Whitmire's living room roommate.

The two did everything together. Mostly drugs. Whitmire was drawn to Carlson because he made her laugh in a world that wasn't funny.

Aaron was also secretly in love with Whitmire. He was jealous when he discovered the two kids sleeping in his living room were a couple. Aaron threw knives at Whitmire one day when Carlson wasn't home, and the couple never returned.

Carlson and Whitmire slept in the cemetery and park bathrooms and, eventually, had a camp on the side of the railroad tracks next to where the old Hunts Tomato Factory used to be. Carlson wasn't reliable. He'd say he was going to "the corner store" and come back three days later, maybe a week later. Whitmire later discovered Carlson had other girls he was seeing, including a stripper who also ended up in prison.

Whitmire admits she had a drug problem. They'd indulge in any drugs they could get their hands on. But Carlson's drug problem was beyond

This is the current view of approximately where the entrance was to the Creek at the end of Lemonwood. The Carlson house was the first one on the left corner. Steve's bedroom was above the garage. *Photo by the author.*

measure. One night, zoned out on heroin, Carlson grabbed Whitmire by the neck and choked her. Nothing prompted it.

The next day, Whitmire told Carlson what he'd done. Carlson cried and apologized. Carlson was a chronic liar. Perhaps this was more manipulation. However, Whitmire insists that this was the only time Carlson was ever violent toward her.

In those days, sober meant they were only drunk, not on drugs. Whitmire's best memories are those rare "sober" days together when Carlson was "ridiculously funny and made me laugh." Carlson took her on several road trips. Of course, a road trip for Carlson meant a stolen truck that he drove, intoxicated, with no license.

They visited Pleasanton several times. Carlson showed Whitmire around his old stomping grounds, including his childhood house, and they drove past the drainage ditch where Carlson's high school classmate had been killed a decade earlier. At the time, Whitmire didn't think anything of the ditch or why they went by it.

About three months after turning eighteen, in May 1996, Whitmire was pregnant. She quit drugs cold turkey. Carlson vowed to stop using drugs as well. He stayed clean for a couple weeks and then fell off the wagon. The pattern continued—a few weeks of clean living followed by another drug binge.

In retrospect, these were the best days of Carlson's life. He would call his mother from a pay phone, tell her about Sarah and the upcoming baby and declare that he'd never been happier. Whitmire remembered the conversation always ended with Carlson begging his mother not to hang up on him.

Whitmire was homeless virtually her entire pregnancy. To this day, she has very bad varicose veins in her legs because she was on her feet the entire pregnancy. There was no resting in bed, even in the final weeks. She'd walk around town, killing time until the cold weather shelter opened each night at 6:00 p.m. She went into labor at a homeless shelter. A stranger called a taxi to take her to the hospital.

On the same day she turned nineteen years old—February 21, 1997—Sarah Whitmire gave birth to a boy. Carlson was twenty-nine years old and now a father for the second time. (Once again, the name of Carlson's child is not being used for privacy.)

Carlson was present for the delivery. A couple days later, Whitmire woke up alone. Carlson was gone. He had stolen the camera with her son's newborn photos as she slept. Whitmire knows he sold the camera for drugs. She has no photos of her son's birth. Whitmire was anemic, lost a lot of blood in the pregnancy and couldn't get out of bed. She stayed in the hospital another four days. Nobody visited her—not parents, not friends, not Carlson.

Once released from the hospital, Whitmire and her newborn baby house-hopped for the next two weeks. Eventually, she had enough money saved to rent a tiny one-bedroom apartment. Carlson moved in, claiming he was clean. Whitmire knew the behavior of somebody on drugs. She thought he was using again. Carlson denied it.

Carlson loved his son and was proud of him. He did some parenting. Carlson changed diapers and fed his son in the middle of the night the milk ice cubes that Whitmire prepared so she could sleep. Carlson took his son on short walks in the stroller and took hundreds of photos. It's evident that Carlson wanted to be a good father. He tried to stay clean; he just couldn't. Drugs were either more important than fatherhood or, more likely, drugs had too powerful a force over his body.

When the child was about six months old, Carlson came home and was obviously on heroin. Whitmire found a bag of meth on her kitchen floor.

Whitmire was horrified that Carlson would endanger the baby. She told him to leave immediately, that she would never jeopardize her child's safe place ever again.

Carlson returned several times, crying and asking for forgiveness. One night, it was raining. He got down in the mud, kissed Whitmire's feet and begged for one more chance. Whitmire held her ground. She didn't let him inside. That's when their rocky relationship ended for good.

When asked, Whitmire said, "I never considered abortion or giving up my child for adoption. He was very special to me and the only reason I got clean. I would be dead right now if having a baby—something to care about—hadn't saved me."

BY THE TURN OF THE CENTURY, Steve Carlson had been an alcoholic and drug junkie for about sixteen years. He didn't have a regular job. He was the father of two children whom he'd completely abandoned. Carlson's mother, Sandra, sent birthday and Christmas presents each year to her granddaughter. They hosted her once in Gardnerville, Nevada, and Carlson's daughter enjoyed the horses on their property.

Over the next ten years, Steve Carlson spent about as much time in jail as he did out of jail. On May 19, 2004, Carlson was arrested for failure to register as a sex offender. On April 1, 2005, Carlson was sentenced to thirty-two more months in prison.

On September 26, 2007, Justine Hamilton passed away at Kaiser Hospital after a long illness. She was extremely ill in her last five years, with advanced liver disease and under constant medical care. She received a liver transplant in 2004 but was never able to manage the side effects and restrictions related to living with a transplant.

"[Justine] was very strange in regard to her addictions," her mother, Janet, said. "I never saw her drunk. Ever. She didn't have any characteristics of somebody who was using any of these drugs. Her skin was good. Her teeth were good. She didn't have track marks."

To this day, Janet Hamilton has never met Steve Carlson's parents, despite persistent requests. The only relative she ever met was Steve's younger brother Richie.

"I tried everything I could think of to come to terms with it," Janet said. "I did not want to lose [my granddaughter]…I got involved in all these support groups to try and understand the appropriate role for me to play. What I learned was, anytime I tried to intervene, it just made things worse."

Carlson learned his ex-wife was dead while in prison. He was served paperwork that his daughter was now in the legal guardianship of her grandmother. Carlson briefly tried to have some friends outside of prison intervene on his behalf. But that was just a one-day threat.

The last time Carlson saw his daughter, she was about eleven years old. It was so long ago that her memories of it are almost nonexistent now. Once she was older, she went into therapy. She did a lot of writing in therapy, mostly about her father's abandonment, and then burned the letters in her cleanse.

ON THE FIRST DAY OF 2008, Carlson was released after another thirty-two months in prison. If he had had any thoughts of starting a new life, they didn't last long. Three days later, on January. 4, 2008, Carlson was arrested on a domestic violence charge. Four days later, on January 8, Carlson was sentenced to another four months in prison.

Carlson was released on May 8, 2008. He made his way to Santa Cruz and lived in the transient community, under bridges and overpasses.

In 2010, Carlson's old neighbor from Pleasanton, Todd Smith, visited Santa Cruz for the day with his wife and two others. Smith had been remodeling a house and invited a co-worker and his girlfriend to join them, a gesture of thanks for his hard work.

The four of them were on the boardwalk when a homeless-looking person tapped on Smith's shoulder. Smith ignored him, thinking it was just a bum looking for money. Then the guy spoke up: "Hey man, didn't you used to be Todd Smith?"

Smith was startled, not knowing how this transient knew his name. He didn't recognize the man. Then the man spoke again; "It's me. Steve Carlson."

"He lifts up his shirt," Smith said, "and he said, 'Check it out, look at my tattoos. I've been in the pen. I molested a fourteen-year-old girl.'"

Smith had previously told his wife about Carlson, his childhood neighbor, and how he always thought Carlson had killed Tina Faelz and how this guy remained in his nightmares. Smith told his wife and the other couple to walk away because they did not want to meet the guy. Carlson kept talking to his old neighbor, bragging about his weed card.

"He was so proud of being in prison," Smith said. "He said, 'Last night, I had this fifteen-year-old girl sucking my dick for pot and a line of crank.' I didn't want to hear it. I had a seventeen-year-old daughter. He told me he'd been in prison for sexual assault or something to a minor. He told me about armed robbery and something else. He was proud of his rap sheet—and his tattoos."

Carlson said to Smith's wife, "We're going to get tattoos around our necks that say 'dirtbags.'"

Smith told his wife not to pay any attention. He told Carlson, "Why would I do that? I don't talk to you. I don't want to talk to you. We're not friends."

A few months later, Smith and his wife were back in Santa Cruz. They ran into Carlson. Again.

"What the fuck?" Smith thought. "That was so crazy and weird to run into him like that again. So freaky. I told my wife, 'We have to get out of here.' I felt like I was going to punch him and then I'd go to jail."

9
THE DNA TALKS

I mean, it sounds sick and morbid, but meth numbs everything.
—*Steve Carlson*

APRIL 5, 2008–AUGUST 2011

The twenty-fourth anniversary of the Tina Faelz murder was on April 5, 2008. It seemed like one of those crimes that would remain unsolved. Married for a third time in 2006, Shirley Orosco contacted the *Pleasanton Weekly* about writing another article. Maybe it would stir memories and get people talking about her daughter again.

Reporter Janet Pelletier wrote the cover story, under the headline, "Who Killed Tina Faelz?" The narrative covered the usual themes of Faelz's difficult life, how it changed the community and the frustration of the police. At police headquarters, case number 84-1496 contained hundreds of pages of reports in five overflowing binders. The list of people interviewed filled fourteen pages. About 350 people were questioned after the incident. Another 250 people had been re-interviewed over the next twenty-plus years.

"Police got a large number of tips, but most of them didn't pan out," Lieutenant Darrin Davis told the weekly. "Students had claimed they were the ones who did it, but it was Friday night party talk."

Davis told the *Pleasanton Weekly* that there were currently four or five "persons of interest" but would not definitively call them suspects. All the

Shirley and her third husband, Ron Orosco. *Courtesy of Karin Reiff.*

men were school age to young adults at the time. Some were in prison, had been released or lived out of state. The name Steve Carlson was never mentioned.

What became most interesting wasn't the article itself. It was the comments left in the online edition. Over forty comments were posted within the first month. A variety of topics were covered. Most were posted anonymously. Three comments loomed over the discussion.

On April 21, 2008, at 11:04 a.m., user 5.0 wrote, "I'd like to see if any of her former classmates have a record. It might be worth looking at."

On April 22, 2008, at 6:43 a.m., user delta said, "I was in her class…I always thought it was a classmate who lived very close to where she was murdered. That guy was always a trouble maker and showed up to school drunk the day it happened."

On October 11, 2008, at 6:20 p.m., an anonymous user simply wrote two words: "Steve Carlson."

Eric Voellm, one of the students who found Faelz's body, posted one of the longest comments on July 22, 2010, at 10:48 a.m. He also publicly accused Carlson by name and included the story of Carlson getting locked in a dumpster a few hours before the murder and how he cut school to drink that day. Voellm also wrote that the guys drinking with Carlson that day teased him, "You're such a loser, you couldn't get laid by that Tina Faelz girl."

That theory (and motive) became the de facto truth for people familiar with the case, especially considering the source was somebody who found the body. During the four years of reporting for this book, that story was repeated to this author many times. Voellm's posting contained just enough truth to be believable. (Those directly involved did not confirm the accuracy of the "you couldn't get laid by Tina Faelz" story, telling investigators they would have remembered that line.)

Katie Kelly also posted numerous comments, including the longest story, sharing details of the harassment she experienced with Faelz, stories about their friendship, their falling out and how much the death impacted her life.

"One thing I can tell you," Kelly wrote, "is that if Tina read this, she'd have a field day. She had no patience for my cries for help, and this is one of them. I think she'd want me to just shut up about it and grow up already, but I can't stop."

Kelly couldn't help it. For over twenty-five years now, she had gone through life pretending that everything was fine. Inside, she asked herself, "Would Tina like me? Am I doing OK? Would she approve?" Or worse, Kelly wondered, "Who is following me? Is there someone in the bushes? In my closet? Am I next? Is it my turn?"

Kelly experienced a recurring nightmare: she is in her house, and Tina is running to her. Tina wants in. Somebody is chasing her. It's cold and raining outside. The wind is blowing trees over. Just before Tina reaches the door, Kelly closes the door.

At age forty-one, Kelly was diagnosed with post-traumatic stress disorder. She went through deep therapy. It brought her an unexplainable peace that she had never previously known. The therapy still didn't bring her friend back, however, and Kelly refused to give up on the case. Kelly was persistent about calling the Pleasanton Police Department to ask if the case was still being investigated.

Another friend with persistence was Stacy Coleman, whose chosen profession of psychology was certainly based on her friend's brutal death.

Kelly and Coleman kept talking about the case—with police, with friends, with relatives, with anybody who would talk about it.

What brought the case back to life, finally, was that the DNA was almost ready to talk.

DANA SAVAGE GREW UP IN ALASKA. She started her career in law enforcement in the city of Escondido in northeastern San Diego County. Savage came to the Pleasanton Police Department in the mid-1990s, spent ten years working as an officer and was reassigned to detective in 2004. Savage worked fraud and burglary cases. Primarily, her focus was sex crimes.

From late 2007 to early 2008, Savage was pregnant with her first child. Unable to do as much fieldwork, Savage devoted her energies to going through the files of two of the three cold cases in Pleasanton. One was simply known as Baby Doe, which remains unsolved. The other was the Faelz murder. Savage had never heard of it.

"What got me really feeling for this girl was when I saw the autopsy photos," Savage said. "That's when I felt really connected to this poor girl. I went through the interviews that had taken place. This was a crazy case, to say the least. There were so many leads it was crazy. It was hard to track what earlier investigators had done because we do things so differently now."

As Savage worked on the Faelz case, Detective Wes Horn from the Dublin Police Department worked on the 1989 disappearance of Ilene Misheloff. Though separated by five years, the locations where the two girls were last seen alive were less than five miles apart, both were using a shortcut through a drainage ditch and both girls had attended Wells Middle School.

Horn and Savage often worked in tandem, going along to interviews together, in case an individual knew something about either case.

Savage talked to Tina's mother, Shirley, and her brother, Drew. Savage reexamined Shirley's ex-boyfriend, his shady friends and the other undesirables whom Shirley knew from frequenting bars. Suspects were compared in the Faelz and Misheloff cases.

The name Steve Carlson surfaced, but only briefly, and more so in the Misheloff investigation. One of the last places that Misheloff was seen alive was the since-closed Foster's Freeze, which was owned by the now-husband of Carlson's elder sister Tanya.

Carlson, however, was incarcerated in Vacaville at the time Misheloff disappeared, due to the lewd and lascivious acts on a thirteen-year-old girl in Davis.

James Knox was a sergeant overseeing the investigation unit in 2007. Knox knew the Faelz case well. He graduated in 1981 from Amador Valley High, the crosstown rival of Foothill High; worked for Pleasanton police as a twenty-year-old Explorer in 1984; and helped search the empty field for the murder weapon the day after the murder.

Lieutenant Davis was transitioning into retirement and recommended that Knox look at the physical evidence in the Faelz case to see if there was testing that could be done.

Savage and Knox arranged for eleven packages to be sent to Crime Scene Technologies, a new private lab located in San Diego, to look for the presence of male DNA. The hope was the culprit had cut himself and left blood at the scene.

On November 1, 2007, criminologist Rupert Page examined Faelz's sweatshirt. It was soaked in so much blood that Page looked for stains away from the central stains to avoid the victim's blood. He identified five different areas that were possibly not the victims. In all the samples, there was either no male DNA detected or there was an overwhelming amount of total human DNA over the possibility of male DNA.

Next, Page examined blood from two different small pebbles found close to Faelz's head. It yielded no male DNA. Finally, Page tried another sample from the bloody sweater. Once again, it revealed a very low level of male DNA.

Scientifically, there was no reason to proceed. The evidence was sent back to Pleasanton.

Savage felt the best piece of evidence was Faelz's purse, which was found in a tree above her body. Savage didn't think the victim would throw her own purse into the tree. She thought it was more feasible the killer did it. Savage consulted with FBI special agent Martha Parker, who regularly assists local departments in crimes against children.

On August 20, 2008, Savage retrieved the purse from evidence and drove it to the Alameda County Sheriff's Office crime lab for DNA testing. Over the next few days, Savage spoke with Jumana Latif, a criminologist at the lab. The Alameda County Sheriff's Office lab wasn't sophisticated enough to handle the complex DNA matter and returned the purse to Savage. Latif recommended the FBI lab in Virginia, which could do a test called MiniFiler.

On September 2, 2008, Special Agent Parker and her partner Claire Duda received the purse from Pleasanton police, locked it in their office overnight and sent it the next day to the FBI lab in Quantico, Virginia. Evidence from other cases—from different agencies throughout the Bay Area—was also sent to the FBI lab.

On September 10, 2008, the purse of Tina Faelz arrived at the FBI lab in Virginia. The case number was 080910011. The 08 stands for the year 2008, the 09 for the month of September and the 10 for the day in the month it was received. The purse was labeled item Q-35.

On December 27, 2008, the FBI received a reference sample of Tina Faelz's blood. It was labeled K-19.

Real life isn't a CSI television show. Results don't come back in hours, days, weeks or even months. In fact, there was so much evidence being submitted for testing, it was almost two full years before anybody at the FBI conducted any work on the purse.

In August 2010, Jacqueline Jarzombek was directed to examine a purse for the presence of a possible bloodstain. At the time, Jarzombek was a biologist at the FBI laboratory in Quantico, Virginia. She examined the purse on Monday, August 16, 2010. She observed four stains on the purse and made the following notes:

- Stain 1—two centimeters by four centimeters; red-brown and brown-black in color; approximately 38 nanograms
- Stain 2—half a centimeter by half a centimeter; red-brown in color; approximately 2.5 nanograms
- Stain 3—one centimeter by one centimeter; red-brown in color; approximately 1 nanogram
- Stain 4—half a centimeter by half a centimeter; light brown in color; approximately 11 nanograms

Jarzombek performed a presumptive blood test on all four stains. All came back positive. Jarzombek only performed a conclusive test, called takayamahemochromogen, for blood on Stain 1 because she could do it and still leave some of the sample behind. For the other stains, Jarzombek felt there was not enough to perform a test and save it for other testing.

Using a scalpel, Jarzombek scraped off a small section of Stain 1, created a microscopic slide and applied a chemical called phenolphthalein. Under a microscope, Jarzombek observed pink crystals, which is a positive reaction for blood.

On Wednesday, August 18, 2010, Jarzombek repackaged the purse and returned it to the case administrator group.

On Monday, August 23, 2010, Lilliana Moreno received the purse and was assigned to collect and extract Stains 1 and 4 from an item labeled

Q-35. At the time, Moreno was a biologist for the FBI, qualified in extraction and certain processes of DNA analysis. Moreno was directed to collect the entirety of Stain 4 and collect a portion of Stain 1.

Moreno did the work on Tuesday, August 24, 2010. She dabbed a little sterile water to an object very similar to a Q-tip, with cotton at the end. That Q-tip was dabbed on the bloodstain until she could see a transfer of the stain. From there, the cotton portion was cut off the swab, placed into a little tube and sealed shut.

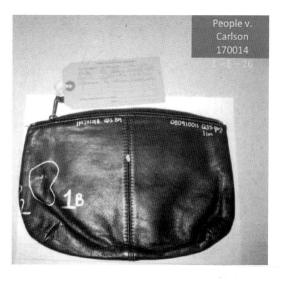

The stain of 1B on Tina Faelz's purse contained the dried blood of Steve Carlson and led to a break in the cold case twenty-seven years after the murder. *Courtesy of the Alameda County District Attorney's Office.*

The tube was incubated. Chemicals were added that burst open the cells. Other chemicals were added to purify the DNA. The purpose of the process is to remove as much as possible from all other detritus in the cell and just clean the DNA off. Once Moreno obtained the extract, she placed it in a refrigerator for the next person in the process. Moreno returned the purse to the case administration group on August 24, 2010.

The purse of Tina Faelz with Stains 3 and 4. Stain 3 matched Carlson's DNA, and Stain 4 matched Faelz's blood. *Courtesy of the Alameda County District Attorney's Office.*

A good profile can be interpreted from just two nanograms. Specific portions of the DNA are amplified (increased in copy number) by a process called polymerase chain reaction (PCR) and then sequenced, generating millions of copies of the thirteen regions of DNA.

On September 3, 2010, the DNA process started on an item known as K-19, the blood of Tina Faelz. Within the next week, Moreno was directed to re-swab a portion of Q35-1A, the biggest stain. Moreno obtained the purse on September 9, 2010, and did the work on Stain 1 on September 10, 2010. She returned the purse on the same day to the case administration group.

On November 15, 2010, the FBI lab was able to get a profile for Stain Q35-1A, with six of the nine locators and the gender. The profile was a male.

IN DECEMBER 2010, STEVE CARLSON's inability to kick his drug habit led to a break in the case that was now twenty-six years in the making. Carlson was arrested in Santa Cruz on charges of possession of methamphetamine and being under the influence of alcohol and opiates. It was a violation of his probation. Carlson had been living in Santa Cruz as a transient.

Per standard protocol, Carlson was required to submit to a DNA test. Carlson's DNA sample was placed in the nationwide Combined DNA Index System, better known as CODIS.

SHANE HOFFMANN IS A FORENSIC EXAMINEr for the FBI specializing in cases that involve nuclear DNA, the standard forty-six chromosomes in which people inherit twenty-three from their mother and twenty-three from their father. Hoffmann oversees the work done by biologists, examines the data and generates the report.

Three possible conclusions are formed: one, a known match; two, inconclusive because there's not enough information; or three, exclusion because no match. The match must be at least one in six trillion to establish a source.

On March 24, 2011, Hoffmann prepared a report on the purse of Tina Faelz, after a CODIS hit was generated by an individual who had recently entered the CODIS system.

The individual was Steven John Carlson.

It was a match but not a robust statistic—roughly a one in one thousand chance it was somebody other than Carlson. That wasn't large enough to make an immediate arrest. But it was enough to restart the investigation, focusing squarely on Carlson, and conduct further testing on the remaining physical evidence.

Finally, the DNA had spoken.

Back in Pleasanton, Detective Dana Savage had been rotated back to patrol and was on injury leave when the FBI called her cell phone with the news the CODIS hit was Carlson. Savage immediately called her supervisors with the news. Inside, her reaction was "dangit."

"I remembered Steve Carlson," Savage said. "At the time, he had an alibi for the investigators before me. Some kind of loose alibi. It was unclear in the report if it was a solid alibi or not. I didn't think it was him. I didn't think it was a kid crime. I thought, wow, from the looks of the autopsy photos, it was such a heinous crime that it couldn't be done by a sixteen-year-old. Knowing what I know now, I see where my thinking was flawed."

KEITH BATT JOINED THE PLEASANTON Police Department in 2001 and became a detective in 2008. He was directed to familiarize himself with the city's cold cases. Batt read through the exhaustive reports on the Faelz murder while realizing it was a cold case that might never be solved.

Then came the phone call from the FBI office in Virginia. The DNA had spoken. It was Carlson. The case was assigned to Batt as the lead investigator, working along with Lieutenant James Knox, a detective supervisor.

One of the first things Batt needed to learn was how much time they had to put the case back together. Batt knew that Carlson was in custody. He asked generic questions to the Santa Cruz Jail authorities to find out the likelihood that Carlson would get released early due to overcrowding or a work credit. Batt was told by the commander that Carlson would be released at the time indicated.

The deadline was Sunday, August 7, 2011.

Batt contacted students, teachers, administrators and neighbors from the 1980s who knew Carlson. He asked for their memories of what happened. He asked if there was anything they knew in 1984 but did not previously tell detectives. He asked if there was any reason why they were not telling the truth in 1984. He asked if being shown a copy of their statements from 1984 would help trigger their memories.

At the end of each interview, after asking people what they knew, he asked them what they suspected.

"Without fail, they said Steve Carlson did it," Batt said. "That continually surprised me."

It surprised Knox, too. Knox had lived or worked in Pleasanton virtually his entire life but was never aware that so many former students thought it was Carlson.

Not all the interviews went smoothly. There was distrust of the police by some of Carlson's former classmates. None more so than Todd Smith, the former friend and neighbor of Carlson who gave conflicting accounts to police in 1984, 1986 and 1988. Smith initially did not want to cooperate when Batt appeared at his door.

"I said, 'Go fuck yourself' and slammed the door," Smith said. "I said, 'I don't want to talk to you. You guys lied to me in the past. Why would I want to help you now?'"

Batt left the house, waited about twenty minutes and then came back and tried again. Batt reasoned with Smith, "This isn't for me. This is for Tina Faelz."

Smith was still livid at the Pleasanton police, but maybe enough time had passed. New detectives were on the force. Smith remembered the sweet girl from his English class, thought about her family and decided to talk. He called his wife at work, told her the police were at the house, reminded her about that guy from his childhood named Steve Carlson and said he would be late for work.

AROUND THE ANNIVERSARY OF HIS sister's death in late March or early April, Drew Faelz would usually surf the web for anything new about his sister's

Drew Faelz and his mother, Shirley, in the 2000s. *Courtesy of Karin Reiff.*

death. Drew would Google Tina's name and type a variety of other terms into search engines to see what results popped up.

In 2011, it was no different. But it was the first year that Drew's wife said something to him about it. She told him, "You need to stop doing this. You get depressed. You start getting quiet. It bums you out."

About a week later, Drew told her, "I *need* to do this. Everything I read online about my sister is all positive. Her friends are on there, making posts on different blogs. I might be quiet thinking about it. But it makes me feel really good."

Little did Drew Faelz know, the police were close to making an arrest.

BEFORE AN ARREST COULD BE MADE, Keith Batt needed another reference sample of Steve Carlson's DNA. The first CODIS hit tells who is the suspect. But that sample cannot be used in court. You need the jail staff to testify how and when they obtained the sample. That is untenable. Batt needed to be able to testify that he obtained the sample from the suspect himself.

On July 26, 2011, Batt and Knox drove to Santa Cruz to visit their suspect in person. The clock was ticking. Carlson was due to get released in twelve days.

The county sheriff's department brought Carlson from jail to the Santa Cruz detective bureau so the interview could be recorded. Carlson was provided coffee and a donut, which he drank and ate. The handcuffs were removed from Carlson's hands. The room was small. There was one door, no windows, one table, a few chairs and nothing hanging on the light-colored walls.

Carlson asked if he was under arrest. He was told no. Carlson asked if he was in trouble. He was told the detectives just wanted to talk with him. Carlson was read his Miranda rights.

Batt said, "You understand you've heard these rights before?"

Carlson replied, "Oh, thousands of millions of times."

Knox and Batt wore suits and ties. They introduced themselves as detectives but did not say from what city. They wanted to build rapport and gain some understanding of how Carlson communicated. They wanted to talk with him as long as possible before they told him the reason they were there. Whatever Carlson might say could help the case.

They asked what had been going on with his life—in the past, in the present and his plans for the future. They could tell that Carlson was curious about why they were there. The conversation lasted about forty-five minutes. Carlson began the interview full of energy. Most of the discussion was about Carlson's drug use.

Among the things Carlson told detectives:

- "Every time I come to jail, I read my Bible and pray that I can quit the drug."
- The jail conditions in Santa Cruz were 100 percent better than Sacramento, and he remarked that he felt like "a Chinese tourist."
- He had overdosed twice on heroin but somehow survived. He now hated all meth addicts.
- He was glad about his recent arrest and wanted jail. He was down to 162 pounds and just wanted to direct traffic down Pacific Boulevard at 3:00 a.m.
- "I hate meth so much. It's taken everything away."
- "I got hep. C. I don't have HIV. And, amazingly, my liver is fully intact."
- He obtained his GED in 2000 or 2001—"And I don't know how I passed the GED. I don't know how I can sit there and read books and everything. And I've been shooting just retarded amounts of methamphetamine."
- Regarding high school: "I just quit going, start ditchin' and didn't fuckin' complete continuation and then just didn't even go."
- "I'm book smart. I'm very, very good—with book smart. I read. I love reading. I could just read. I wanna read about everything. And I take a creative writing class on Friday. And it's like when I write, that's my emotions."
- On his family: "I haven't been in contact with them for twenty years. My family are strangers and I don't, like, wanna go there right now. Nothin' definitely, I just—that's a closed book. I appreciate we go on to somethin' next 'cause I don't even want to go into that. It's emotional for me."
- "I'm surprised how I'm opening up to you guys…And uh, don't think I'm some sucker just because I'm getting emotional. I mean, I'm not. I mean, I'm tryin' to be cooperative with you guys."
- "Lot of cops think like I'm some con. Or not—not a con—but I can be one and I know how to be—manipulate people very well, but that's just because being in the system, you gotta manipulate what you need to get, you know what I mean?"

Carlson said be began smoking marijuana at age fourteen (the seventh grade) and started using acid and psychedelic drugs by age sixteen (his freshman year in high school). He told them he was battling an addiction to methamphetamine that began when he was sixteen. Hyper because of a thyroid condition, Carlson said the drug calmed him initially but also ruined his life.

By age twenty, Carlson told the detectives, he was an everyday user, taking doses heavy enough to kill most people. Carlson told the detectives he came from a middle-class family and his parents had no idea how to handle him or his drug use.

"Meth numbs everything," Carlson told them. "Your kid could die in front of you and you do a big ol' shot of meth and you're like, 'Oh, uh, well, clean it up.' I mean, it sounds sick and morbid, but meth numbs everything."

Boom. That was the type of bombshell statement the detectives were hoping to hear. Satisfied they had the background information they were seeking, the detectives told Carlson they were from Pleasanton and had come to talk about the 1984 murder of Tina Faelz.

Carlson started to cough, almost like he was going to throw up, although nothing came out of his mouth. Carlson's body language changed dramatically. His answers were much shorter. The detectives tried to probe him for information. Among his responses:

- "That was a hell of a long time ago."
- "It's a cold case."
- "I don't know how much I remember about that. I [unintelligible] you can ask the psychology—I—and I—I've been on psych meds but, I mean, I have had no—I don't even remember some [unintelligible]. I'm not being dumb, what do you want me to tell you?"
- "How long ago was that anyways?"
- "You drove all the way down here for [unintelligible]?…Wow."
- "I remember, I went, I went to a boys' camp. I went to a boys' camp and then after that, I, uh, left Pleasanton. So I was like seventeen."
- "It was like right across the street from my house."
- "I don't remember nothin' about that."

Batt asked Carlson to submit a DNA sample. Carlson did not want to do it. Batt had a search warrant, so Carlson didn't have a choice. Batt handed Carlson a swab and asked him to circle it inside his cheek. Carlson complied, doing the swab twice. Batt placed the two samples into sterile envelopes.

Back in Pleasanton, Batt locked the samples of Carlson into evidence so the saliva could dry overnight. The next day, Batt overnighted the samples to the FBI lab in Virginia.

Carlson was less than two weeks from getting released. Time was critical. Normally, the FBI doesn't do cases like the Tina Faelz murder. That's a state case, not a federal one. Usually, the FBI gets involved if it's a potential serial killer or something involving multiple jurisdictions. But the FBI made an exception on this cold case that was twenty-seven years old.

Martha Parker—the FBI agent from the Oakland office who was the liaison between the Pleasanton Police Department and the FBI lab—explained the circumstances and requested the evidence get tested immediately as part of her local agency cooperation.

On July 1, 2011, Tina Faelz's purse was resubmitted to the FBI lab.

On July 25, 2011, all the remaining blood evidence of the purse was tested on all the stains in order to obtain a more robust statistic.

On July 28, 2011, the FBI lab received the buccal swab from inside the cheek of Steve Carlson, labeled as K-22.

Hoffmann, the FBI forensic examiner in Virginia, generated a second report on the four stains found on the purse, the blood sample of Faelz and the K-22 DNA swab from inside Carlson's mouth. He compared the results of the two reports. A second independent DNA examiner reviewed the case to see if there was an agreement. Then a third review, also independent, was an administrative review for paperwork.

The sample for the Q35-1 stain on the purse was a match to Carlson. Hoffmann calculated the odds the stain on the purse was somebody other than Carlson were 1 in 4.6 quadrillion for an African American, 1 in 15 quadrillion for a Caucasian, 1 in 5.7 quadrillion for a Southeastern Hispanic and 1 in 11 quadrillion for a Southwestern Hispanic.

The approximate current population of the world is 7,000,000,000.

Here is what 1 in 15 quadrillion looks like: 15,000,000,000,000,000.

The samples for Q35-2 and Q35-3 did not generate enough of a robust sample, because all nine DNA locations didn't align, but the bloodstains also matched Carlson's DNA.

The Q35-4 sample was also not robust enough for a complete DNA profile. But none of the numbers were different from the reference sample of Faelz's blood. Hoffmann calculated there was a 1 in 150 million chance that Q35-4 was a Caucasian female other than Faelz.

The only blood on the purse belonged to Steve Carlson and Tina Faelz. The DNA had spoken. Still, the work was just beginning for prosecutors.

10
THE ARREST

I may be a dirtbag, but I didn't hurt nobody.
—*Steve Carlson*

SUNDAY, AUGUST 7, 2011

Steve Carlson, now forty-three years old, had completed a nine-month sentence on a drug-related charge. Since the three years he spent in prison for lewd and lascivious acts on a child under fourteen from 1989 to 1992, Carlson had spent roughly two decades in jails and prisons, almost as much time as he'd been a free man.

Carlson was estranged from his family. He wasn't aware his mother had died five months earlier. He was estranged from both children he fathered. He didn't have a home or anyplace to go except the streets. He would be just another transient in Santa Cruz, with a threatening vibe that frightened locals. His teeth were decayed from drug use, and his body was covered in menacing tattoos. However, if he was being honest with himself, Carlson knew what was coming.

Detective Keith Batt and Lieutenant James Knox drove to Santa Cruz in the early morning, getting breakfast in the beachside city, and then sat in the lobby of the Santa Cruz County Jail. They waited for Carlson to get officially processed and released. They saw Carlson walk into the lobby holding his personal property.

Batt and Knox approached Carlson. Each officer grabbed one of his arms and put them behind his back. Knox uttered the sentence that is the highlight of his thirty-plus years in law enforcement: "You're under arrest for the murder of Tina Faelz."

Carlson did not scream in protest. He did not proclaim his innocence. His response was, "OK." On the drive to Santa Rita Jail in Dublin, Carlson slept for about forty-five minutes of the one-hour drive.

Batt and Knox visited Shirley Orosco at her home on Virgin Islands Court in Pleasanton. Upon seeing the officers, Orosco asked, "Did you find him?" Their smiles provided the answer. Orosco told the officers she had a feeling that day.

The detectives had a lot of phone calls to make. One of them was to Ron Penix, the biological father of Tina, still living in Washington.

"I was extremely grateful and yet heartbroken at the same time," Penix said. "There's just evil in the world. There's nothing you can do about it…I wish that I had appreciated [Tina] the way fathers are supposed to appreciate their daughters. Fortunately, I've been able to do that with my other two daughters and granddaughters, to make up for the horrible father that I was."

Current police chief Dave Spiller called the former police chief Bill Eastman, who went through so many sleepless nights trying to solve this case that hit so close to home, so Eastman would not get blindsided by a reporter's phone call. Did Eastman ever think, "What did we miss?"

"No, we've been over that so many times," Eastman said. "Intellectually, you know that you did everything that you could have done. Not me, the group. The human resources were poured into that case. There was nothing left to do. To reopen it so many times with people ignorant to the case, so they can reconstruct. I knew we did everything that we could do. I never felt we missed anything. There was no expense spared. I never got any bullshit from the city about over-spending and going nowhere."

The police told the media they'd have a major announcement to make the next morning about a case from 1984.

AUGUST 8-10, 2011

What happens when your estranged brother is arrested for an unsolved murder that happened twenty-seven years ago, essentially across the street from your childhood house? That's what Tanya Pittson, Richard Carlson and Amy DeMarino were about to find out.

The Pleasanton Police Department publicly announced it had made an arrest in a cold case from 1984. It couldn't say the name of the suspect because he was sixteen years old at the time of the crime. Reporters and amateur sleuths were able to easily do an inmate search and determine that Steve Carlson had been transferred to Santa Rita Jail and was being held on the charge of murder.

The memorial tree for Tina Faelz, planted in 1984, was moved closer to the parking lot after the school was renovated. Friends and family placed fresh flowers after Steve Carlson was arrested in 2011. *Photo by the author.*

Former classmates posted links to articles and photos on Facebook. They clicked, liked, poked, commented and shared. They read old articles, from before the arrest, and commented more. They talked on the phone, at work, on e-mail and in coffee shops and bars. Neighbors brought fresh flowers to Tina's memorial tree and plaque on the high school's campus.

You couldn't go very far in Pleasanton, or anywhere in the East Bay suburbs, without finding people discussing the unusual case. The common responses from the former students at Foothill High were "We always knew it was him" and "What took them so long?"

Steve Carlson's siblings weren't totally surprised. Soon after arresting Carlson, Batt went to the Dublin home of Carlson's elder sister Tanya so he could interview her before the press reported the arrest.

Amy disconnected her phone in advance so she could avoid calls. Her close friends from childhood couldn't reach her. She had barely spoken to any of them since the arrest. Amy learned that police wanted to speak with her. Amy was not going to defend her brother, not after what he did to her in the 1980s. Amy called the police herself from a hotel room in Florida. She had no evidence that Steve was innocent or guilty, but she told police about her childhood, including how Steve molested her.

An overhead view of the neighborhood as it looks now: A is the crime scene location; B is the exit that students in Valley Trails went through to return home; C represents all the houses that did not exist in 1984, it was an open field; D is the entrance to the Creek; and E is the Carlson home. *From the author's personal collection.*

Richard was on vacation. When he returned to work, colleagues noted the same last name, similar blond hair and tried to casually ask if they were related. Richard bluntly asked co-workers if they had something specific to ask.

Tanya's different last name provided less obvious attention. She noticed one co-worker would bring up the topic, she'd steer the conversation another direction and the co-worker would steer it back to the story in the headlines. Tanya was not willing to discuss the case with co-workers, reporters or neighbors for years.

The first time Tanya visited Steve at Santa Rita Jail, he didn't recognize her and thought she was a reporter. Maintaining his tough-guy jail persona, Steve faked a jump into the window toward his sister.

Tanya told him, "That's going to get you nowhere. That hasn't worked for you all these years. You have to stop playing into that, 'Yeah, I'm creepy.'"

August 11–September 30, 2011

Sarah Whitmire was living in New York when she found out her son's father had been arrested for the murder of a cold case from 1984. At the bottom of an article on the *Pleasanton Patch* website, Whitmire posted a series of anonymous messages. The only editing done is a little grammar.

> *I have long ago estranged myself and my dear son from him due to his erratic behavior and drug abuse. He was never violent toward me, nor did he display other violent behaviors such as kicking, throwing or breaking things. Although he would lash out verbally, he never harmed a hair on my head physically. He has many mental ailments, including ADHD and a stress disorder, which he would sometimes take prescription meds for. But most of the time, [he] opted to self-medicate. He had many intolerable behaviors, but believe it or not, he always meant well in his heart. He never got help for his mental disorders. Being a severe addict, this took precedent over his ability to better his life. Steven was also known for lying. The lies he told were stories told with the intention in his messed up brain to make him look like a badass because he had no sense of self-worth. He would make up stories about beating up or stabbing people who he never harmed. This made him feel like people would respect him by fearing him.*

Janet Hamilton, the mother of Steve Carlson's deceased ex-wife Justine, didn't know about the arrest until contacted by this author in late October 2011. Over the holidays, Janet told her granddaughter about the arrest. It's possible she had already heard from others. Carlson's first child didn't have a dramatic reaction. She wasn't mad or upset, and she didn't burst into tears. Her father had been out of her life so long, and her memories were so vague, that she pretty much didn't care.

Jon Adler learned of the arrest on Facebook. Adler witnessed Carlson's drinking and drug use in the late 1980s and early 1990s. Adler saw the physical damage that Carlson inflicted on his first wife, Justine, the best friend of Adler's ex-wife Tracy.

"Everything made sense," Adler said. "Now I get it. Now I know what was driving this twenty-two-year-old to drink himself to death. We all knew it was something. We didn't know what it was."

THE JUDGE PLACED A GAG order on the case, preventing the participants from talking to the press about any details of the case. But when reporter Eric Louie from the *Contra Costa Times* showed up at Santa Rita County Jail, Carlson granted him an interview.

"I may be a dirtbag," Carlson told Louie on August 11, 2011, four days after he was arrested, "but I didn't hurt nobody."

Carlson told the reporter he didn't remember much of his discussions with the police in 1984 or how he felt about the crime. He said he drank and did drugs a lot. Carlson said he saw Faelz around Foothill High but didn't know her personally.

In the jailhouse interview, Carlson said he was planning on attending Cabrillo College and becoming a counselor. Carlson admitted he was estranged from his family, due to his drug use, and did not talk to his two children.

Carlson told the newspaper he had no idea why he was being charged. He figured that he was an easy target to close the cold case because of his criminal record and heavy tattoos. Carlson wasn't aware of the evidence the police now had and said he didn't say anything when the police re-interviewed him recently.

The article concluded with Carlson denying that he used to admit to the murder to other students in the 1980s. When asked about the sex offense in the 1990s, Carlson told the reporter he simply hooked up with a fourteen-year-old girl at a UC Davis fraternity party.

(Jessica Hart, the eyewitness to the attack, says Carlson's story is "bullshit. I was there. I saw what happened. It was behind the dorms on UC Davis campus. It was just the three of us. He was buying us liquor and obviously trying to get us drunk. I was thirteen. She was thirteen. He was twenty-two. Not only was she underage, she was extremely underage.")

JOHN CARLSON GRANTED AN INTERVIEW with the *Pleasanton Patch* a few days after his son was arrested, on the condition that his name was not printed. No such agreement was made for this book. John told reporter Tanya Rose that he and his wife, Sandra, were in Tahoe on the day of the murder. John said he and his wife returned home to Pleasanton that night and police were "all over" their house. (His memory was slightly off. They returned the next day.)

The father said police searched the house, asking if they could go into the attic, and crawled up there looking for a weapon. John stated that his wife looked over Steve's clothes and didn't find anything suspicious—and they never saw a knife, that day or ever. (There's no record of police searching the house.)

When asked in 2014 why her mother was looking through Steve's clothes, Tanya said, "I don't know if she was looking because she thought maybe it was Steven or if she was looking because it was so close to the house." Tanya even asked her mom, "What are you doing?" and the response was, "What if somebody had come around? I just want to make sure."

John Carlson also told the *Pleasanton Patch* that his son and another friend had seen Faelz's dead body lying in the culvert that day and then Steve ran home and called his grandmother.

When asked why Steve would call his grandmother, Tanya said, "She lived in San Leandro and she was just a part of our life. He probably didn't know the number of our parents. He knew her number and wanted to call somebody. She couldn't recall for sure the timing of that. I remember, for some reason, it stands out in my brain, I was thinking that it was a little after four o'clock."

In 1984, police talked to all the students who were around the crime scene—Eric Voellm, Jay Dallimore, Tony Fisher, Todd Oelsen and Todd Smith. None of those five students indicated that Carlson was with them. There's nothing in any of the exhaustive police reports that any police officer spoke to Carlson on the day of the murder.

Even after the police stopped talking to Steve Carlson in 1984 and 1986, John and Sandra Carlson were not immune to hearing the ongoing rumors about their son.

"That was him trying to make everyone think he was cool or something," John told the *Patch* in 2011. "Kids say all kinds of things. I think he thought people would think he was a big man, and I don't think a lot of people believed him. I don't know why he would say that. What was he thinking?"

The police re-interviewed all of Steve's siblings in 2011, separately, about the night of the murder. All three told investigators the parents didn't return home until the next day. All three said they slept together in their parents' room, but their memories differed on which room Steve slept in.

Tanya Pittson is adamant that police were inside their house on the night of the murder, using the bathroom and drinking the coffee that she specifically brewed for the officers. She says they were not looking around the house for evidence.

"They were using the bathroom," Tanya said. "They were coming in for coffee and using the phone. It was before cell phones. I know for sure they did. They were there. I felt better they were there. I felt uneasy because there was a murder across the street from the house, and my parents were gone. It made me feel good."

Police Chief Bill Eastman and Lead Investigator Gary Tollefson deny that police were inside the Carlson house on the night of the murder. Three additional detectives who would testify at the trial also said they did not go inside the Carlson house and didn't see any other officers inside the house. If it happened, it was never included in any of the police reports.

If Tanya is correct, the police would have reason to lie or mislead. If they were inside a house on the night of the murder and it turned out it was the house of the killer, it would be embarrassing that they missed him.

On August 16, 2011, this author wrote a letter to Steve Carlson in jail. On August 26, 2011, a letter arrived in the mail. It wasn't from Carlson. It was from Ronald L. Marks, a self-described "fine jailhouse lawyer." Marks wrote a six-page, handwritten letter on yellow paper. Marks also included a letter that Carlson sent him, which Carlson signed by his prison name, VOID.

Ron

Good afternoon!! thank you for your advise. You are right. I have been treating this whole thing like a joke. Because that is what it is. I'm _completely_ and _fully_ innocent. That's why I'm probably treating it so unserious. Anyways I have no interest in helping this guy out writing his book. I had a bad childhood. Nothing _weird_. Just _not happy_. I don't wish to relive all that drama. Now I live for that day when they say I'm absolutely not guilty. Because of them tampering with evidence. And I sue them. Don't trip. I'll even buy you some new teeth (haha). Some "gold ones". Serious bro. Have a blessed day. Because I'm having one.

All my respects.

VOID

11

THE CURIOUS CASE OF TODD SMITH

I prayed to God, "Don't let him say it was me and him." I was not there. I was nowhere near there.
—Todd Smith

OCTOBER 2011–OCTOBER 2012

This was unknown territory for Aundrea Brown, the first public defender for Steve Carlson. She had never seen a forty-three-year-old man in juvenile court. Brown argued successfully that because her client was sixteen years old at the time of the murder, the case needed to abide by juvenile court protocol. That meant a behavioral assessment that is standard for juveniles being considered for transfer to the adult court.

Carlson's second public defender was Richard Foxall, who represented Carlson before Judge Trina Thompson on October 14, 2011, for a contempt of court charge stemming from Carlson's jailhouse interview with the *Contra Costa Times*.

Foxall was five months removed from another high-profile murder case from Pleasanton. Professional poker player Ernest Scherer III was sentenced to two consecutive terms of life in prison without parole for murdering his parents at their Castlewood Country Club residence. Scherer was deeply in debt and trying to collect his inheritance.

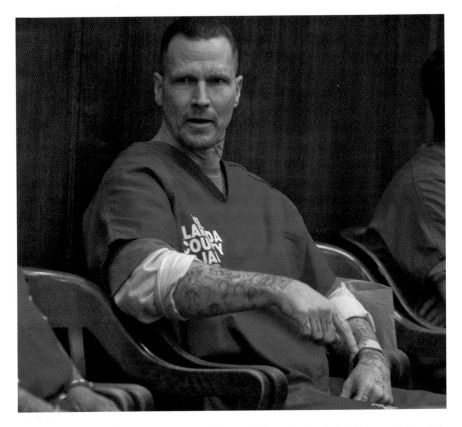

In 2011, Steve Carlson appeared in juvenile court before a judge decided he would be tried as an adult in the 1984 killing of Tina Faelz. *Courtesy of the Bay Area News Group.*

Tanya Pittson wanted to make sure Carlson, her younger brother, received a fair trial. She wasn't impressed with Foxall and sought new counsel.

"[Foxall] made reference that he didn't really want this case," Pittson said. "He told my brother that he would get a [plea-bargain] deal. I wrote a really scathing letter to the judge that I didn't want him."

Tanya didn't want a lawyer from the East Bay area who already knew the case. She wanted an outsider to provide an objective defense. Tanya settled on Cameron Bowman from the South Bay firm of Valencia, Ippolito and Bowman to take over his representation. Carlson's family paid for the new lawyer.

According to the bio on his firm's website, Bowman earned his undergraduate degree and law degree at Santa Clara University. Bowman was originally a Santa Clara County prosecutor before switching to criminal defenses for sex crimes, domestic violence, drug crimes, driving under the influence/driving while intoxicated, white-collar crimes, theft, assault and felonies. In 1998, Bowman was named Santa Clara's Trial Attorney of the Year.

Bowman needed time to review the case, so Carlson remained in the juvenile court system through the end of 2011. Bowman's lead investigator was fascinated by the case, uncovering one weird story after another wacky angle. Pittson praised Bowman's firm for the amount of discovery they uncovered on her brother's case.

On January 10, 2012, a fitness hearing was held, and Alameda County Superior Court judge Rhonda Burgess ruled Carlson would be tried as an adult. Burgess cited the degree of criminal sophistication exhibited in the killing, the severity of the crime and previous failed attempts at rehabilitating Carlson, among other considerations.

On March 6, 2012, Carlson formally entered a plea of not guilty. The preliminary hearing was set for seven months later.

OCTOBER 16, 2012

Judge Larry J. Goodman presided over the preliminary hearing in *People of the State of California v. Steven J. Carlson* in Department 107 of the Rene C. Davidson Courthouse. The preliminary hearing has no jury. The judge does not decide guilt but, rather, if there is enough evidence to force the defendant to stand trial, using the "probable cause" legal standard.

Carlson's preliminary hearing included testimony from the pathologist who performed the autopsy on Tina Faelz in 1984, Lead Detective Gary Tollefson from the initial investigation, forensic examiner Shane Hoffman from the FBI office that oversaw the handling of the DNA and the newest lead investigator, Keith Batt.

The most interesting testimony—and most controversial—was from a former friend of Steve Carlson. It continued the curious case of Todd Smith. At 10:41 a.m., Smith took the witness stand. For the next thirty-six minutes, Smith provided gripping testimony about the day of the murder and shocking statements about a conversation the next day. The details of Todd Smith's testimony are as follows:

- Smith was a childhood friend of Steve Carlson, growing up as neighbors. They were in the same grade, although Carlson was one year older.

- Smith was in a freshman English class with Tina Faelz at the time of the murder.
- Smith saw Carlson the day of the murder, before lunch. Carlson was trying to start a fight with a senior football player. Carlson kept provoking the player, who told him to sleep it off. Carlson's behavior was not normal. Carlson had been drinking. All of Carlson's actions were slurred. Carlson was dancing in a fighting motion. It was one person Carlson was trying to fight. He was almost falling over.
- Smith saw Carlson get thrown into a large dumpster by football players, and then the lid was locked. They flipped the dumpster on its side and rolled it. About ten to twenty people were watching this in a crowded area.
- A janitor unlocked the dumpster, and Carlson was released. He was angry and upset. Food and garbage were on him. Carlson got out and headed away from campus, in the direction of his home.
- Toward the end of lunch, Smith and three other students went to make sure Carlson was OK. They walked to his house. Carlson no longer had his dirty clothes on. He was cleaned up. It did not appear he was still drunk. Smith and the other three boys went back to school.
- After school ended, Smith got on his moped and was riding around campus and the neighborhood with Weldon Mann. Smith said he dropped off Mann at the school on his moped and went back home.
- Smith said he saw Carlson outside his house, backing his mom's car out of the driveway. Smith got into the car with Carlson. Smith was in the passenger seat. Carlson was driving.
- Carlson said he wanted to go to 7-11. Smith didn't want to go. They started driving to 7-11 on Muirwood Drive. They saw Tina Faelz walking toward the Creek area. Carlson said, "That's Tina." They were less than thirty feet away from Faelz when Carlson said the victim's name.
- Carlson turned the car around and drove back up Muirwood at a high rate of speed, way too fast. They never went to 7-11.
- Carlson dropped off Smith at the front of the street. Smith got out and went home. Smith didn't recall where Carlson went next.
- Smith went home and got on his moped again. Smith drove around the neighborhood and picked up his younger brother, Brent, at Lydiksen Elementary and brought him home.
- When Smith was on his moped, two kids in a higher grade came out of the Creek and said there's a body in there.

- Smith took his moped home because he knew the cops would be coming, and he didn't have a license for the moped.
- Smith ran to the body with other neighbors. He mentioned all three of the Oelsen brothers (Todd, Troy and Travis) and said maybe Art Guzman or Todd Fisher was there as well.
- Smith said the body didn't look real. He saw so much blood inside the clothes. The body was facedown. He used his shoe to nudge the body, near the shoulder, about an inch or two. He realized it was really a person. The boys came out of the Creek screaming and yelling to call 911.
- Smith said he saw Steve Carlson in his front yard. The police were not there yet. Carlson was not messy or dirty. He was wearing clean clothes. His hair was wet or greasy. He hadn't been like that at school. Carlson was wearing shorts or swim trunks.
- Smith told Carlson there was a body in the Creek but that he didn't know who it was. Carlson told Smith he was not going down there. Smith felt it was odd because if there was anything exciting, Carlson wanted to know and see it.
- Smith told a story of once being at Carlson's house for a pool party. Carlson turned on the garbage disposal and threw a live lizard into it.
- Smith then told a story of Carlson grabbing cats by the tail, flinging them around and saying, "Look, I caught a possum," as the cats would scream.
- Smith said he heard Carlson say twice that he didn't want to go down there.
- When the police showed up, Smith said he talked to the police and went into the interrogation room until midnight.
- The next day, Todd and his brother, Brent, were on their dirt bikes in the neighborhood. They saw Carlson in front of his house. Carlson was smoking marijuana with his younger brother Richie. Steve was also sucking air out of the gas tank of his mom's car.
- Smith said he was twenty feet away and his younger brother, Brent, was ten feet from Steve. Steve chased down Brent and said, "Come here little boy. Let me kill you, like I killed her."
- Smith said he punched Carlson, and then he and his brother went home on their bikes.
- Smith said he called the Pleasanton Police Department. They had left a card with him the previous night. Smith didn't recall which cop he talked on the phone. The response was "Thanks, kid"…and they essentially blew him off.

After a fourteen-minute break, Cameron Bowman began his cross-examination of Todd Smith at 11:31 a.m. Bowman systematically tore apart Smith's version of events. Numerous times, Bowman gave copies of police reports from the 1980s that contained statements that Smith gave at the time. Bowman questioned Smith about specific statements from 1984 that were completely the opposite now.

Judge Larry Goodman admonished Bowman for his editorializing at one point, telling the defense lawyer, "This isn't Santa Clara County." Sitting next to her father in the courtroom, Tanya Pittson briefly questioned her decision to hire somebody outside of Alameda County.

Bowman toned down the editorializing, but he maintained his aggressive questioning of Smith. Among the next highlights that were learned:

- In 1984, Smith told police he was walking with Weldon Mann on Aster Court. Mann asked what time it was. It was almost 3:00 p.m. Mann left to meet his mom at the top of the school. Carlson caught up with them at 3:02 p.m. In 2012, Smith did not recall saying that.
- In 1984, Smith told police he rode around the neighborhood on a moped with Carlson just after 3:00 p.m. In 2012, Smith did not recall saying that.
- In 1984, Smith told police he and Carlson went back to Smith's house at 3:17 p.m. In 2012, Smith did not recall saying that.
- In 1984, Smith told police he went inside his house and called his mom at 3:20 p.m. In 2012, Smith did not recall saying that.
- In 1984, Smith told police he saw boys in the field who were burnouts or stoners. In 2012, Smith *did* recall saying that. It was one of the few statements that Smith did recall.
- In 1984, Smith told police that he and Carlson were back inside their house, and two guys said there's a dead person in the Creek. In 2012, Smith did not recall saying that.
- In 1984, Smith told police he was with Carlson the whole time. In 2012, Smith did not recall saying that.
- In 2012, Smith said he did not recall being in the car with Carlson and two detectives on Wednesday, April 11, 1984, as they retraced their steps from the day of the murder. Smith said he had some memory of the police driving him around but not with Carlson.
- In 2012, Smith said he was trying to be truthful in 1984.
- In 2012, Smith said he picked up his younger brother, Brent, from Lydiksen Elementary School. When he got back home, people were

saying there's a dead body. Smith said he went to see the body with brothers Todd and Troy Oelsen and Tony Fisher. Smith said he spit up when he saw the body.

Repeatedly, Bowman asked Smith why he didn't tell the police any of the information that he had just testified over the previous twenty-something years. Smith's response was that he tried to tell the police, and they wouldn't listen to him.

- In 2012, Smith read the report from Detective Saulsbury after they talked on April 17, 1984. Smith had no memory of this conversation, which was the third time police talked to him in the twelve days after Faelz was murdered.
- In 1984, Smith told police that he rode around on a moped with Andy Hartlett and Weldon Mann. In 2012, Smith did not recall this.
- In 1984, Smith told police he also saw Mike McCord before he saw Mann. In 2012, Smith did not recall this.
- In 2012, Smith was told Pleasanton police had no record of the phone call Smith allegedly made after Carlson said "I'm going to kill you little boy" to Smith's younger brother. Smith replied he was positive it happened, and he punched Carlson as a result.
- In 2012, Smith said he didn't recall if Detective Tollefson re-interviewed him in 1986.
- In 1986, Smith told police he didn't remember the details from 1984 because it had been a long time. In 2012, Smith did not recall that conversation.
- In 2012, Smith testified that he told Detective Keith Batt, "I'll wear a wire. I'll go get him. I'll beat it out of him." Smith said he was frustrated at the time.

"So, we should trust you even though you don't remember being interviewed four times?" Bowman asked Smith. "Is it possible after twenty years this just popped into your head?" Bowman finished his scathing cross-examination of Smith at 2:52 p.m.

Next was Detective Gary Tollefson. Under cross-examination, Bowman tenaciously went back to work at discrediting Smith's version of events. The highlights of what Tollefson testified are as follows:

- Todd Smith never pointed the finger at Steve Carlson in 1984 or 1986.
- If a phone call was made by Smith about an encounter in the neighborhood that involved a confession, he would have followed up on it.
- Along with Detectives Fracoli and Saulsbury, they re-interviewed Todd Smith in 1986. Smith told the detectives his memory from 1984 was hazy because it had been a long time.
- If Smith had told him that Carlson had wet hair or swimming trunks within an hour of the murder, Tollefson would have included that in his report.

As the day was nearing its end, Bowman sat down next to his client. Carlson quietly said to his lawyer, "That was awesome."

OCTOBER 17, 2012

The second day of testimony in the preliminary hearing did not go as awesomely for Steve Carlson. FBI forensic scientist Shane Hoffmann testified in clear detail how the evidence was received in the FBI lab, the process of amplifying the sample and the results. Hoffmann testified, "I can say to a reasonable degree of scientific certainty that Steven Carlson is the source" of the male blood found on Tina Faelz's purse.

Bowman continued his strong questioning, this time on the reliability of the blood evidence on the purse. Bowman alleged that Pleasanton police misplaced the purse from April 1984 to January 1986.

"Nobody knows where this purse was until 1986," Bowman said.

Prosecutor Annie Saadi told the court the purse wasn't in the Pleasanton police logs for those twenty-one months because police didn't examine it until January 1986, when they checked it for the first time for blood and fingerprints.

During the closing arguments, Bowman argued that Smith was not a credible witness, and his testimony should be disregarded. "For two years, [Smith] essentially provided the alibi for Steve Carlson," Bowman argued. "It's only in 2011 that Todd Smith says, 'Oh, by the way, it's Steve Carlson?' It's crazy. It makes no sense. Steve Carlson was a sixteen-year-old student. He decided one day after getting drunk that he's going to commit murder? Then while drunk, he's going to shower and get rid of a murder weapon?"

After closing arguments were made, Alameda County Superior Court judge Larry Goodman said the testimony of Todd Smith was "problematic." However, Goodman ruled that Carlson should face trial on the murder charge because of the DNA evidence presented.

This case would be decided, almost entirely, by a small dried stain of blood on a purse that had sat in an evidence locker for over twenty years.

March 8, 2015

Two years and five months later, Todd Smith reflected on his day on the witness stand. That day, Smith was so sick he couldn't drive himself to court. A police officer drove him.

Smith has dealt with severe blood clots since 2010, which impact his eating, sleeping, breathing, ability to work longer than two hours and ability to go to the bathroom. Hundreds of veins attached to his liver and grew to his esophagus. The veins are bleeding internally. One day, the veins will burst, and he'll have about two minutes to live. He's met with seven specialists. He was told there's no cure. If Smith is still alive in five years, he'll consider it a miracle.

In the days leading up to his testimony, Smith was scared that Carlson would suddenly change his story, plead guilty and claim that Smith helped him kill Faelz. "I cried myself to sleep so many nights before going to court," Smith said. "I prayed to God, 'Don't let him say it was me and him.' I was not there. I was nowhere near there. I passed the lie detector test anyway. I had nothing to do with it."

Smith was not expecting or prepared, mentally or physically, for the grueling cross-examination. He's still glad that he went, even if his testimony was inconsistent. He wanted justice for Faelz. He knew his information needed to be told, that he held crucial information to the case. Smith just wishes he'd have stood up for himself more.

Smith explained, "Steve's lawyer said, 'Why didn't you do something more?' What am I supposed to do? I'm fifteen years old, man. I did call the police and they said, 'Thanks kid,' and hung up on me. That was it. The lawyer said, 'How come that's not in the police reports?' I don't know why it's not. I wish I would've responded like that."

The first time Smith was interviewed by police, in 1984, he now admits what he told them was a lie. It's Smith's biggest regret because his lie became Carlson's alibi.

"That's my neighbor, that's a kid my age," Smith explained. "Wherever he was, no problem, I was there with him. That's the only thing that I could have been thinking. I know there were times that I was not with Steve. I know that for a fact. That day, I thought no way could Steve have killed her. Once I realized it was a real body that I turned over, that was such a brutal thing. There's no way a sixteen-year-old kid could do that…I guarantee you the police thought that too. I'd have bet any amount of money a sixteen-year-old kid couldn't do that. No way. Not even Creepy Carlson. It wasn't until he tried to stab my little brother, faking a knife motion. He was smoking a joint with his brother Richie and breathing gas out of his mom's car. He said, 'Let me kill you like, like I killed her.' I knew it was him. Right then. He didn't go see the body that day. I knew in my heart that he did it."

12
MOTIVE?

I was Carlson's first. I was his training.
—*Jane Doe*

Pleasanton police had DNA evidence that Steve Carlson's blood was on Tina Faelz's purse. What they did not have was a motive. They did not necessarily need a motive. Motive is not required to get a guilty conviction in court, but it sure helps. People ask why. They're used to hearing about motives on TV shows. Some jurors might need to know "why" before they can vote "guilty."

As Detective Keith Batt went through the police reports from the 1980s and put the case back together, one name stood out. It was a person that Batt needed to find to get a side of the story that had been missing for three decades. Batt tracked her down. She was fragile and initially reluctant to talk. Eventually, she agreed to tell her story.

Batt learned the police didn't really interview her in 1984. They thought they did. But in reality, they were interviewing her younger sister. In a five-hour interview, the woman laid out shocking details that police had never known. A few classmates knew some of the story in the 1980s and gossiped about it, but they did not know the complete story. Only a handful of people previously knew the whole story that you're about to read.

Tina's friend agreed to tell her story for this book. Due to the sensitive nature of what she experienced, her name will not be used. Instead, she'll be called Jane—as in Jane Doe. This is her story, as told by her, through a series of interviews that lasted well over four hours.

I met Tina in the eighth grade. I can tell you that I didn't like her at first. Only because the way she befriended me was to tug on my hair, to kick me, to punch me and giggle and walk away. I was a little confused. I didn't get it. Every day, she did that to me. Pull, kick and punch me—really hard. It would make me mad. I would chase her. She was good at running away. But it was so playful. By the time I got to her, I couldn't hit her. I wasn't that type of person. I think that was her way of becoming my friend. If I didn't hate her and kick her back, she became my friend. She did it to other people, too. They would get really angry and chase her around the fields. They would actually push her and hurt her. That was her way. I thought she was strange. That's not how I made friends. But that's how she made friends.

Tina would sometimes purposely not take the bus home to Pleasanton. I would say, "Bye" as she got on the bus, but I didn't want to see her go. She'd jump off the bus. She never asked if she could come to my house. She would just purposely get off the bus and follow me home. My house was right across the street from the school. I'd say, "Mom, I have a friend, can she stay and have dinner?" And she did. We became closer that way. I don't know how often we did that. It was at least once a week.

From what I understand, she wasn't even watched at home. She was just left alone. I didn't know anything bad about her home life, other than it seemed like she was always by herself. I didn't even know she had a little brother until the funeral. That's how we became friends, and closer friends, when she started staying at my house. My father would take Tina home at a decent time. I don't remember even talking to her mom about it at all. I don't remember asking her, or calling her, if it was OK. But Tina said it was OK. She never got in trouble the next day, so I guess it was OK with her mom. We have some pictures of her playing Scrabble with us.

The best time I did have with her was when she invited me to her birthday party, a sleepover birthday party. That was my best and most wonderful experience. We toilet papered Katie Kelly's house. We looked for things in the neighborhood, a scavenger hunt. That night, there were some boys playing tricks at her door and doing doorbell ditches. Somebody put a bag of doo-doo and lit it on fire. That was the most traumatic thing I'd ever seen at that age. I couldn't believe they did that to her. That creeped me out.

If it weren't for Tina having this thing with knives, I don't think she would have gotten killed. Whatever I say to you, I don't know what it means. All I can tell is how I feel and what I'm thinking. The first time I noticed it was at her house. We were making lunch. She took out one of the biggest knives in her drawer. She was pretending to be a ninja warrior. She was being very dangerous about it. I was very afraid of knives. I had a phobia of knives. She was just flailing it around and pretending to jab me with it or poke me with it. She scared the shit out of me.

It ended up turning into she had a fascination with knives. She came to my house and pulled out my knives. And she pretended to be a ninja again. She'd throw the knife in the air. She was dangerous. I feel funny telling you this. But this is what she did. It was almost like she didn't have any boundaries in getting hurt. I tried to tell her, "You're not supposed to play with knives like that." She was pretending to be showing off, like a karate expert.

I can name, honestly, two times that she did that—for fun. Once at her house and once at my house—for fun. The third time, I don't remember if she had a knife, but that's when she was trying to scare Steve Carlson away.

I can't tell you exactly the first time I met Carlson. I know it was at Wells Middle School. He was in one of my classes. He sat behind me with his friends. I remember a lot of snickering and giggling and laughing. He put little pieces of paper in a straw and spit them at me, trying to get my attention. I don't know why he picked me. This boy that I hardly knew was always standing in front of me. It wasn't a boy that I liked.

My first actual contact with Steve, he got me behind the backstop of the ball field. We were supposed to be on the grass. We weren't supposed to be that far behind the backstop. You couldn't see us back there. That's when it first happened. It was during lunch recess. I thought we were going to sit and talk. But it wasn't that. It was a struggle. It's not like I screamed. I was always the quiet one. I didn't want to cause any trouble, so I stayed quiet. Then when it finished, it wasn't anything different. I was already getting abused by my father. I thought it happened to all the girls. I thought it was my time. I let it go. I didn't want anybody to know. He wasn't my boyfriend. He was my rapist.

Oh boy, I can't remember how often it happened. It felt like every day for the first three months of the school year. It was quite a few times, to the point where it got easier and easier not to fight and argue.

We went to my house at lunch. My mom worked a lot and would come home for lunch about half the time. She would ask me why I'm home at lunch. There were a few times I had to hide in the closet when my mom came home. It was pretty scary. I was not allowed to have boys in the house. I remember two times, clearly in my head, that Carlson was there when my mom came home. I was terrified that my mother would find him. I didn't want her to know I was having sex at that age. I didn't even know what sex was, really, until later.

Carlson forced himself into my house. He went inside through windows that I couldn't break into. I couldn't do it. He knew how to break into my house. No matter how much I hid, he came inside the house. He was pretty tall. That scared me. I kept freaking out. Carlson probably thought it was consensual after awhile, when I stopped pushing back. I didn't want to fight. I kept quiet. I made sure if my mom walked in the door, I wasn't screaming when he was forcing himself on me.

One day, Tina asked me what was going on. Carlson had a schedule, and I followed it. If I didn't go, he threatened to tell my family and friends what was going on. I told Tina I had to go, and she couldn't come to my house. She asked, "Why not?" I just told her there's a bad person in my house. She asked, "Who is it?" I told her. She forcibly followed me to the house.

I hate this part. She ran with me across the street, when the yard duty was not looking. I told her, "You're going to get in trouble." I begged her not to come. Carlson was trying to break in. Tina said, "No no no no, he's not allowed in the house." I think she put the garage door down. I locked the back door. There was a lot of kicking of the garage door, more kicking, screaming. "I'm going to kill you. You better not come in here." Those weren't Tina's exact words. It's been thirty years. But this was a direct threat to Carlson to not come into the house. I'm pretty sure she had a knife. The feeling I had was there was going to be danger and a fight.

Tina was very eager not to let him inside the house. She caused a huge commotion. I thought the yard duties would hear her. It scared me. I let him inside through the backdoor because I was trying to turn down the volume of what was going to happen. I let him inside. I told him, "Please do not hurt her. Don't touch her." Tina was still angry that he was inside the house. I wanted the situation calm. My neighbors could hear it and call the police. I was terrified of what Carlson would do to her and me. I said to Tina, "Wait here." I took him to the back room. She wanted to know what's going on. Of course, he tried to make her do things that she wouldn't do.

The next day, Tina stayed away. Maybe she thought we were boyfriend-girlfriend. I didn't want to explain he was raping me. I just wanted him to stay away from her. I hope you understand. I felt it was the right thing to do. I didn't want anything to happen to Tina. I tried to play it off, as a game. I begged her not to come across the street because then they would meet. I told

Tina I didn't like him in the house, and that's why she got angry. I don't know if she had any idea what was going on. I know she watched him come to my house. She stayed back, except that one day. She had to find out what was going on. He asked her to lift her dress up and stuff like that. I didn't want that. I just closed the door. I wanted him to finish his business and be on his way. He was very forceful. Wrestling, choking, everything, to get me in the position he needed me. It didn't matter the position, especially the first time behind the backstop. As gross as it may sound, I knew it was not normal. My father was at least nice. Carlson wasn't nice. But that's because I fought. I fought and fought until I couldn't fight no more.

Tina and I never talked about it anymore after that.

Toward the end of the school year, Carlson brought over five boys to rape me. They were his good friends. I guess I was easy, at that point, to break their virginity. I just lay there. I did whatever Carlson told me to do. I had no control. I remember the names of the boys. I told Detective Batt their names. There were other boys waiting outside too. But there's only forty-five minutes at lunch. I wasn't screaming. The five boys he brought in, they knew what he was doing. I'm sure he told them I was the easiest girl ever. My reputation continued in high school. I swore not to be with any other boys after that, to prove that I was not easy.

After junior high, he was completely gone. It was like a phase. I never thought of him stopping by. He was only there because the school bus brought him there. Tina and Carlson went to Foothill High. I went to Dublin High. I remained friends with Tina, even though we weren't in the same school.

That year, when we were freshmen, I heard something similar might be happening to Tina. I thought it was odd that she was hiding it from me. There was always something being left at the door, even the trick with the doo-doo at her birthday party. That didn't seem right to me. Tina would do things in the neighborhood the kids didn't like, like TPing their house. There was a lot of commotion in the back of the house. I was terrified. What's going on? Tina started giggling. She thought it was funny that they were trying to break into the house. All I knew was my situation was similar. Are they doing it because she's my friend, and they're trying to do the same thing to her? I don't know. I wasn't there all the time. She told me these boys are trying to break into the house. That bothered me.

When I first told her I was in karate class, she got so excited knowing. The first thing she did was take out a knife and play with it. I said, "Woah, Tina, stop. You're going to slice me. That's not how you do it. We teach you self-defense. It's not to attack people." Later that day, I was very clear on getting her into karate class. I told my father. I think it was the next day. This is when she was visiting my house regularly, staying at my house until after dinner. The next day, we took her into my uncle's karate class and showed her what it's like. All my cousins and I were yellow-purple belts. My sister was just starting, so it was perfect. It was exciting. I couldn't wait for her to start karate class with us.

A few days later, she was murdered. I don't remember how I found out. No one really told me. Maybe I saw it on the news. I think my boyfriend at the time told me. I didn't think Carlson killed her. I thought it was completely unrelated to what Carlson did to me. Even when an unknown person, some boy, came to my house and tried to convince me the killer was Carlson, I was still dumbfounded. I was just like, "Why even tell me that? I could care less. I don't want to have anything to do with Steve Carlson. All I know is my friend is dead and how would Carlson have anything to do with it?" This was months later, after the murder. I guess the impression I was getting is there were so many rumors going on at Foothill High they wanted to let me know about it.

I ran away at age fourteen. It was about a month or two after Tina was killed. My younger sister stayed at home. When I called, she would update me on the situation at home. My parents knew I ran away. There was no missing child fliers or anything. I wasn't missing. I was a runaway. The police I'd run into, they knew where I was. They were my friends. They knew my situation at home. That's when I went to a foster home. I think at age sixteen is when the authorities found me and put me in a house, both me and my sister. In order to rehabilitate my father, we weren't allowed to be at the house. Then we had to have counseling with my father, just to bring us back into the home. I think that was around age eighteen.

How did I survive? That's a good question. To summarize, I just walked forever. I ran into people like me, and sometimes I'd sit there and talk about the same things and the devastation of my life. I'm a wanderer. I don't know how I survived. I had an old boyfriend in high school who taught me some street smarts, how to ask for free food at restaurants. I ran away to the city for awhile, but it was with somebody watching my back. I came back to my hometown, where I felt safer. The streets of Dublin were my home. I just hung out with my friends. When it was time to go to sleep, I'd stay at my friends' house sometimes. I could go to my cousin's house anytime. I could just never stay at my house after what happened with my dad.

I didn't tell anybody what Carlson did to me or what my father was doing to me. I had one lady that I finally opened up on my secret. If it wasn't for her saying how important it was to tell the police, I wouldn't have done it. I didn't want to get in trouble. I was going against my father's wishes.

I think I would have rather been dead back then. I was a lost child, so lost, a rebel, trying to find a place, a home. I tried going to live with my aunt and uncle. But the whole idea of embarrassing the family came up. When my auntie called and said I should have never said anything, that blew me away. That was just a shock. That I put a bad name on my family. They somewhat banned me from going to family functions. I broke the silence. It's been a lifelong thing, the incest that's been going on, for who knows how long in my family. The family is still battling. I still get a lot of stares. I'm the daughter who told the police on my father.

I have post-traumatic stress disorder. I have quite a few traumas. I have what you call those memory flashbacks. My relationships are damaged. If it wasn't for me going to medical school for awhile, I don't think I'd be able to handle this. I have a high sensitivity level. Now I can sense a creep a mile away.

My dad is now a registered sex offender. You know how people say, "You can't change a person"? I think my dad has changed. I love him dearly. If it wasn't for my dad, I wouldn't be able to understand the world. There's two sides of my father. One side I wished I never knew. The other side was my father, the father he should be. It was my mother who I had the bigger problem with…She pushed the truth away. I found out my grandfather was molesting her. That was her secret. But it's not a secret with me.

When Detective Batt came over and told me Steve Carlson was arrested for murdering Tina, my jaw dropped. Everything hit me. Everything just made sense. Detective Batt told me to be prepared for the long, drawn-out court system. I did. The whole time, I was ready to go up there and take the stand myself and testify whatever I had to.

I was Carlson's first. I was his training, per se. If he could do it to me, he could do it to as many girls as he possibly could. When I found out he did it to another girl, I couldn't believe it. I wish I would have said something. But I didn't. My story was more with my father. I didn't bring up Carlson as my rapist. I don't know why. My family was more of an issue. I didn't want my parents to know. To this day, my parents don't know what Carlson did to me.

I'm not sure the message I want to send to Tina's family. I'm not sure if it's an apology or what. I haven't talked with them since the incident. My heart melts and goes out to them. Sometimes, I just want to hang out with them. I want to tell them about all the fun we had together. I've blocked out a lot in my life. It's been so long. In my head, I made it out like it never happened, my girlfriend is still in Pleasanton, and someday I would see her again. It's still unreal. It's in a dream state. Maybe it's closure for me, if I talk to the family. I went to the funeral in 1984. It wasn't enough. I feel huge love toward them. I hope they know how much love I have for Tina. She was the best friend I ever had. I've never been able to find anybody close to her. I've had no best friends since that happened. A few friends, but nothing as special as I had with Tina. All the crazy, weird, scary things she liked and taught me—even TPing a house was crazy, and I did it with her. She showed me things I never did as a kid. She was magical to me. I think about her every day. I feel like I've been through a dozen lifetimes. It's always been in the back of my head. I always felt she was there with me.

On the day Tina Faelz was found murdered, one of the books found near her dead body was *Flowers in the Attic*, a 1979 novel by V.C. Andrews. The book is a gothic horror/family saga that includes significant incest by the main characters. It was banned in certain schools because of the incest.

The book was not part of the curriculum at Foothill High, so Faelz was reading the paperback on her own. Maybe it's just coincidence. The book has sold over forty million copies worldwide. Or maybe it's not just coincidence that Faelz was reading a book about incest, knowing that one of her best friends was getting raped by her own father.

One of the toughest decisions for the district attorney's office was whether to put Jane on the witness stand. Her testimony would not be clear motive, but it would be a possible motive. Jane was the only person who knew about the day Carlson wanted to get inside her house and Faelz was screaming to stay away while holding a knife.

Carlson and Faelz weren't known to interact very often. One day, they had a verbal altercation on campus. Three decades later, some recalled that Faelz was defending Jane's honor, while others believe that Carlson was trying to get Faelz to perform the same acts Jane did.

About a dozen students and a couple teachers were aware, or later became aware, of the Carlson-Jane angle. The "dopers" from 1986 discussed this theory and told the police. However, the word "rape" was never used. Back then, it was just thought that Jane was a promiscuous young girl.

For those who know a portion of the Carlson-Jane angle, they've always wondered what impact that had on the events of April 5, 1984.

Did Faelz tell Carlson to leave her friend alone? Did Faelz threaten to tell police or school officials about what Carlson was doing to her friend? Was Carlson initially trying to charm Faelz back to his house? Was an intoxicated Carlson trying to use force to coerce Faelz back to his house? Was Carlson one of the boys who were trying to break into Faelz's house that school year? What words were exchanged that prompted Carlson to snap and viciously stab Faelz forty-four times?

Or was all this a coincidence? Was the socially challenged Carlson oblivious that "no means no"—or did he think Jane enjoyed it because she stopped protesting? Was Carlson guilty of being an overly aggressive pervert but innocent of murder?

An investigator for Carlson's defense went a step further, asking questions to see if it was Jane's father who might be responsible for Faelz's death. The theory was that Faelz was going to tell the police about Jane getting raped by her father. However, no evidence exists that Jane's father had anything to do with Faelz's murder.

As it turned out, jurors would never hear any of the information presented in this chapter. This book is the first time Jane's story became public knowledge.

Prosecutor Stacie Pettigrew wasn't confident the judge would even allow the testimony. Surely, the defense would have vehemently argued to keep the information from being allowed in the courtroom.

Even if the information was presented, it wasn't a concrete motive. Nobody knows with certainty if that's why Carlson killed Faelz—if he killed her. Knowing Jane's fragile state, Pettigrew decided it wasn't worth asking a woman now in her forties to relive the humiliation of her teenage years on the witness stand and then get subjected to cross-examination from Carlson's lawyer.

Moreover, Pettigrew did not want the murder trial to turn into "Did Steve Carlson rape Jane?" Pettigrew wanted the case to remain focused on "Did Steve Carlson kill Tina Faelz?"

13
THE TRIAL

My sister went through thirty years of hell.
—Karin Reiff

FEBRUARY 13, 2014

Shirley Orosco's life was forever changed when her daughter was murdered on April 5, 1984. She was already having a difficult time coping with a bizarre divorce. The violent, unsolved death of her daughter caused her mental health to deteriorate.

Neighbors and family members told stories of Shirley's irrational behavior. Once, Shirley was seen trying to pull a child out of her car at the Shell gas station next to the 7-11 where she used to work. In reality, nobody else was in the car. Stories abound of Shirley having an argument with an imaginary child. Shirley's family tried to check her into a mental hospital at one point.

Shirley's relationship with her family fluctuated over the years. Sometimes, she leaned on her siblings and parents for help. More often, she pushed them away and became further withdrawn. One of the few constants in her life over the next thirty years was the hope that her daughter's killer would eventually be found.

On the day Steve Carlson was arrested, in her heart, Shirley knew the police had the right culprit. Maybe this was a mother's intuition. Maybe this was confidence in the detectives and the evidence they presented to her. Or

Shirley Faelz and her daughter, Tina, in the early 1970s. *Courtesy of Karin Reiff.*

maybe this was just what you do after three decades, when it's the last thing missing in your life—you believe this is it, this is the one, and you convince yourself that intuition is fact.

Shirley welcomed this author into her home about a month after the arrest was made. She gave her blessing to the book, provided names and phone numbers of friends and family members to contact and encouraged the project. Shirley called this author numerous times over the next two years, usually out of the blue, to say hello and ask if the book was still happening.

"I'm going to be ready for the trial," Shirley said frequently. "That's my goal. I want to hear the verdict. I know it's him. I need the closure."

During the phone conversations, it was evident from Orosco's voice, and her random thought patterns, that her health was not improving.

Shirley Faelz poses with a framed photo of her daughter in the late 1980s. *Courtesy of the Faelz family.*

Carlson went through two public defenders, his sister paid for a well-respected lawyer for his preliminary hearing and the county appointed a new lawyer for the trial. Four different lead prosecutors were handed the case. All these changes in lawyers meant further delays. The new lawyers needed time to review the thousands of documents in the case. Schedules needed to be cleared for judges and lawyers. Delay after delay did not help Shirley's fragile body.

On February 13, 2014, *People of the State of California v. Steven Carlson* was scheduled to begin. In truth, the trial was not going to start. It had already been pushed back, again, until October. But that was the day circled on the calendar of Shirley Griffiths Penix Faelz Orosco.

That was the day Shirley died, at age sixty-six, of a sudden heart attack.

Shirley's sister, Karin, went through some belongings after the death. She found photos the family hadn't seen in thirty years, along with a poem that Shirley wrote on the one-year anniversary of her daughter's murder.

"My sister went through almost thirty years of hell after Tina's death, and I think she finally died of a broken heart," Karin Reiff said. "The photos of Shirley with Tina show how happy [Shirley] was before someone came and ruined her life. I truly do feel that if Tina had not been murdered, Shirley would be alive now. Thirty years of the stress and pain finally killed her. The murderer should be up for two murders as far as I'm concerned."

AUGUST 2014

In the summer of 2014, the DNA unit in the Alameda County Prosecutor's Office completed a big rape kit backlog. It received a significant number of hits. Those cases needed to be worked and investigated.

Stacie Pettigrew was brought into the DNA unit to focus on murders. She inherited the Faelz case in late July 2014. Pettigrew was in the middle of another high-profile case, the 2012 Oikos University mass murder that killed seven at the Korean Christian college in Oakland. Pettigrew took the case to a grand jury, and it was finished on August 20, 2014.

Two days later, Pettigrew started working on the Faelz case—about one month before the Steve Carlson trial was scheduled to begin. The discovery had over 3,600 pages for Pettigrew to quickly review.

Pettigrew needed to decide if she would put Todd Smith back on the witness stand, after his testimony was termed "problematic" by a judge at the preliminary hearing. She didn't know if the defense would call Smith, since he provided the alibi in 1984. She decided against having Smith testify.

Despite dozens of former students claiming they heard Carlson confess at various parties or make cryptic comments, Pettigrew decided not to put any of them on the stand. Nobody heard it directly—or was willing to say, definitively, that they heard it directly. It was always secondhand. Not to mention, the case had been discussed at such length at parties, in the press and all over Facebook that memories were tainted by these discussions. The testimony might not hold up over cross-examination.

"I tried to track down anybody who heard that firsthand," Pettigrew said. "The police did, too. Either nobody wanted to be a snitch or everybody else was drunk. It's a difficult case because everybody always says they always knew he did it. But nobody had firsthand knowledge."

Pettigrew would only put one student on the witness stand who was a Foothill High student in 1984: Katie Kelly, the best friend of Faelz who was in the midst of a schoolgirl falling out. Pettigrew would rely on the adults from 1984, now mostly retired, to provide the basic facts of the school, the area, the murder, the investigation and all the testing that had been done over the years.

Overall, Pettigrew's strategy was to narrow the focus. She was going to rely on the DNA. It was always all about the DNA. For twenty-seven years, there hadn't been enough evidence. The only reason this case was finally going to trial was DNA.

It was going to cost at least another $80,000 for Cameron Bowman's firm to continue representing Steve Carlson through the end of the trial. The Carlson siblings and father had to weigh the cost of Bowman's firm against the likelihood of getting a not-guilty verdict with such strong DNA evidence. The hard part was done. Bowman's investigator had already compiled all the background information.

Carlson's family decided not to retain Bowman.

The court appointed Annie Beles from the firm of Beles and Beles to defend Carlson. According to the firm's website, Robert J. Beles started his own law firm in 1979. His daughter, Annie, began working for the firm in high school—after school and during vacations—answering phones, organizing files and doing whatever grunt work was needed for clients. In 2007, the State Bar of California certified Annie Beles as a criminal law specialist.

On September 25, 2014, Judge Clay refereed as Pettigrew and Beles argued about what information was admissible in the case. Beles wanted the

DNA evidence from the purse thrown out, which would thereby dismiss the entire case. Beles's argument to the judge was:

> *Not all DNA is OK. And some DNA should not come in because there is a complete void, abyss, bottomless hole of evidence as to how this DNA got onto the purse. We are talking about an absolute minuscule amount of blood. We are talking about less than a 25th of a drop of blood, not in a drop pattern. It's so small that it's not even in a drop pattern; it's in a smear pattern. And that is the amount of blood that could easily come from a school desk where they have the same class, a wall, a locker, a garbage can, a lunch table that Steven Carlson was sitting at, had a hangnail or a bloody nose or got beat up and put into a dumpster, put a little blood. There is no way that the prosecution can say that this happened only at the time of the murder, in a certain way.*
>
> *I think that this is the line. I'm sorry a fourteen-year-old girl was stabbed. I'm sorry that they don't have the evidence to prove it. But the DNA evidence causes—invites so much speculation, invites so much burden shifting that the court should draw the line now and the court should exclude it and—which would, therefore, I believe, require dismissal.*

Beles also motioned to deny the admission of the DNA based on the chain of custody. Judge Clay allowed the DNA blood evidence to be used in the courtroom. Beles tried to get everything that Carlson said to detectives in 2011 dismissed. Judge Clay allowed certain portions of the interview to be heard by jurors. The lawyers and judge went line by line through the transcripts to decide what would be eliminated.

Originally, Beles asked for makeup foundation to cover the tattoos on Carlson's forehead and neck from the jury, so they would not be prejudiced by his looks. However, after the judge allowed the video of Carlson's interview to be shown, Beles decided it would be bad strategy to have the jury see his tattoos on the video and then covered up in court.

There was a spirited debate over whether the jury would hear about Carlson's drug use, which started around the time of the murder.

Beles said, "I don't even know the words to state as strongly as I feel that whether or not a sixteen-year-old boy starts using drugs and that a teacher thinks that he's going downhill is not probative that he killed someone. And I think that we're running right up against just a full-on character assassination: He is a weird kid, so he must have done it?"

Judge Clay allowed the timing of the drug use to be used. Among the other rulings by Judge Clay on September 25, 2014, were:

- The lewd and lascivious acts on the thirteen-year-old girl in Davis, and Carlson needing to register as a sex offender, could not be used as evidence.
- The jury would also not hear about Carlson's twenty-two years in the system, at least four felony convictions, his hepatitis C or the fact that he was taking psychological medication.
- Wood shop teacher Gary Hicklin would be allowed to tell the story of Carlson getting locked in the dumpster on the day of the murder, that Carlson was strong and that Carlson told him "only God knows" who killed Faelz. However, Hicklin was not allowed to testify about the brutal beating Carlson gave another student shortly before the murder, that Carlson showed zero emotion at the memorial or that he was a sneaky kid who was good at manipulating people.
- Physical education teacher Susan Klas would not be allowed to testify that Carlson went downhill after the murder, not participating in class, isolating himself, cutting class, being late to class, not taking a test and lying about being in class.
- Carlson's statement to police in 1984, which is printed on pages 67–68 of this book, a detailed description of where he was at each moment on the day of the murder, was not allowed. However, Carlson's statement to police in 1986 that he joked about killing her, but didn't really do it, was allowed.
- Former assistant principal Jack Keegan could establish the timeline for the detention that Faelz skipped, that the boys who found the body were in detention and that kids used the tunnel as a shortcut to get under the freeway. However, Keegan would not be allowed to give his opinion of Carlson, that Carlson got into a fight after the killing, that Carlson was troubled and got suspended or that Carlson talked viciously to girls.

Beles was very concerned that witnesses would make statements along the lines of "I heard from so-and-so" because it was such a well-publicized case from a small town so long ago. Judge Clay reminded Pettigrew of the importance of witnesses sticking to material that was only from their direct knowledge.

OCTOBER 14, 2014

Thirty years, six months and nine days after the murder of Tina Faelz, opening statements were delivered in *People of the State of California v. Steven J. Carlson*. It was three years, one month and seven days since Carlson had been arrested.

Stacie Pettigrew, the deputy district attorney and lead prosecutor in the case, began her opening statement by standing in front of the jury and counting.

Pettigrew counted from one to seven—"We will never know the order in which her horrific injuries were inflicted, but those were the slicing-type wounds to her face and to her head." Pettigrew then counted from eight to eleven—"Those were the defensive wounds to her hands while she was either fighting him off or trying to protect herself." Pettigrew then counted from twelve to thirty-eight—"Each of those deep stab wounds were inflicted to the back side of her body, probably while she was facedown on the ground, and each and every single one of those stab wounds were inflicted while she was still alive." Pettigrew then counted from thirty-nine to forty-four—"Those wounds were inflicted after she was dead."

For the next hour, Pettigrew laid out the prosecution's case—the condition of Faelz's body, why she was in that culvert, where the defendant lived, all the police's attempts over the years to solve the case, the confessions by the defendant over the next two years at parties and the advances in DNA technology.

"For twenty-seven years, he got away with murder," Pettigrew told the jury, "until science caught up with him."

The first words Beles told the jury were, "Steven Carlson didn't kill Tina Faelz. This is an unsolved murder. It was an unsolved murder in 1984, it was an unsolved murder in 1986, it was an unsolved murder in the 2000s and it remains an unsolved murder. That is what the evidence will show."

Beles showed a photo of a smiling sixteen-year-old Carlson and reminded the jurors *that* kid is on trial—not the older, tattoo-covered man in the courtroom that day. Beles told the jury that Faelz and Carlson attended the same middle school and high school and that they knew each other because the schools were not that big.

"They can't tell you how it happened," said Beles, adding that 1984 "is not the dark ages. There are a number of forensic techniques with which the Pleasanton police were familiar but did not utilize."

Beles told the jury that in 1986, "a young, goofy Steven Carlson is interviewed by the police officers not once, but twice over two days, for hours at a time, to discuss these alleged rumors. And what Steven says is, 'Yeah, I joked and said that I killed Tina. A lot of us boys did.'...He's not developed as a suspect because they realize any of the rumors must have come from him making these ridiculous, poor taste jokes."

Beles told the jury that in 2008 "they finally say that there is DNA on the purse. There will be no evidence how it got there. It will be pure speculation."

Beles told the jury that in 2011 "there's a national database. Out pops Steven's name. That's not good enough for the FBI. They want to do another testing. They go back into these infinitesimal amounts of blood. They come back with what is a fuller DNA profile. They run this swab again, and they consume all of what they took off the purse. Therefore, it is untestable (again). But what DNA evidence in this case cannot ever tell you is when it got there or how it got there. It can also not tell you whether it was contaminated necessarily."

And finally, Beles told the jury, you won't see or hear from the prosecution anything about motive, fingerprint, method, weapon, sequencing or timing.

"What you're going to hear," Beles said, "is some bold-faced statement that it must have been Steven Carlson."

GRISLY, BLOODY PHOTOS OF Tina Faelz were shown on the overhead projector, from the crime scene and from the autopsy table. Less than an hour into the first day, Drew Faelz couldn't take it anymore, excusing himself from the courtroom after seeing photos of his dead sister.

"It was one of those things that you know it's going to be gruesome and scary," Drew said afterward. "You do want to look, but then I didn't want to see them. Some of the pictures were OK. Then I just started thinking about how she didn't deserve anything, and then I remembered what my mom went through, and I remembered how my mom had to sit by my door for months to help me fall asleep. I told my cousin that I'm feeling nauseous. I was looking down and I see sweat drops hitting the floor."

Steve Carlson rarely looked at the bloody photos of Faelz on the projector screen. He'd steal a glance, every once in awhile, but didn't look very often. Carlson showed little emotion all three weeks of the trial. He'd occasionally whisper something to his lawyer or write something on a piece of paper. He rarely looked at Faelz's family. He didn't look at the jurors or study their reactions. The jury mostly avoided looking at Carlson as they entered and exited the courtroom.

The prosecution called thirty-five witnesses over nine days. The defense called none. The defense considered calling Tanya Pittson, which is why she didn't attend the trial, but decided against it. Closing arguments were made on Tuesday, October 28, 2014.

Pettigrew told the jury about the blood found on the purse:

> *It's indisputable that his blood is on Tina's purse. It's indisputable that her blood is on her own purse. It's indisputable that nobody else's blood is on her purse. It's indisputable that nobody else's DNA, fingerprints, hairs, sperm, semen, any biological material is on any of the evidence at the crime scene. And it's indisputable—I'll even give it to you that he joked that he killed Tina, but you have no evidence of anyone else joking that they killed Tina…The only reasonable conclusion is he left that blood on her purse when he killed her.*

Pettigrew also reasoned to the jury about the circumstantial evidence adding up:

> *You'll reach a point, and that point could be different for all of you, but you will reach a point where it's just one coincidence too many. And the only reasonable interpretation from all of the evidence is that he's guilty of the murder of Tina Faelz, that his blood could have only come from this incident when he brutally, viciously murdered her.*

In her closing arguments, Beles told the jury:

> *This case isn't about headlines. This case isn't about snippets. It's not about sound bites. It's about critical thinking skills with the evidence that has been presented to you. Not speculation. Not conjecture. Not "I'll guess." Not "probably." It's about the facts that are presented to you in this case. Any time that you are asking the question in deliberation of, "Well, what else happened? Who did it? Why didn't they do this? Then why didn't he explain? How else did the DNA get there?" All of those things are putting the burden on the defense, and that is not what the law is.*
>
> *The time is now for the doubt. The time is not tomorrow. The time is not next year. The time is right now. Look at yourself in the mirror and say, "Can I actually convict this guy on a cough and on a purse with some blood that I don't know how it got on there?" No. "Can I honestly look at myself in the mirror and say I have an unwavering conviction—abiding conviction—of the truth of the charge?" No, no. You do no justice to Tina Faelz and her family if you convict the wrong person.*

Once the closing arguments were made and the jury began its deliberation, it was certainly possible that Carlson would suddenly become a free man. If so, where would he go? The last time he was out of jail was 2010, and he was a transient living in Santa Cruz.

In the days leading up to the verdict, Steve talked about getting tattoos and girls with his dad in Nevada. But his father didn't want him living there. The younger siblings, the twins, definitely wanted no part of their older brother. By default, did that mean Steve would come home with Tanya and live in her home?

Steve told Tanya he just needed a little push and then he'd be all right on his own. When Steve was in the Santa Cruz Jail, he was planning on becoming a counselor for drug users when he got out. Tanya thought he was lying. She looked into it, and he had actually filed some paperwork to make it happen.

Tanya sheepishly admitted that she didn't want Steven staying at her house. She paid for his defense because he was her brother and everybody deserves a fair trial. But it's not like they were close. They hadn't spoken in almost twenty years before he was arrested. And regardless if Steve was innocent or guilty of a murder from thirty years ago, that didn't change the type of person he'd become.

John Carlson and Tanya Pittson decided, if the jury found Steve not guilty, that they would get him a hotel room for a few nights—and then discuss further options.

On Wednesday, October 29, 2014, jury deliberations began. The foreperson selected was a scientific engineer. At 8:39 a.m., the jury asked for the tape of Carlson's interview. They broke for lunch and left at 1:30 p.m. for the day.

On Thursday, October 30, 2014, the jury arrived at 8:30 a.m. and reached a verdict a little before 11:00 a.m.

The foreperson read the following:

> *We, the jury, in the above-entitled case find the defendant, Steven Carlson, guilty of a felony, to wit: Murder in the first degree, a violation of section 187(a) of the Penal Code of California, in that on or about April 5, 1984, in the County of Alameda, State of California, said defendant did unlawfully and with malice aforethought murder Tina Marie Faelz, a human being, as charged in Count 1 of the Information.*

Faelz's supporters greeted Pettigrew with exuberant cheers and emotional hugs. Some members of the jury also stayed around for about an hour, visiting with the family and hugging them as well.

"I always tell the families, I do what I do for you," Pettigrew said. "There's nothing I can do to bring your loved one back. My whole goal is to bring them—I don't use the word closure anymore—a finality to the court process. There's no feeling like that. Truly. I was telling people, 'I always connect with my victims' family.' But there was something different about this case and having them wait thirty years. The gravity of it was enormous."

A 1979 Christmas card featuring Tina Faelz and her younger brother, Drew. *Courtesy of Karin Reiff.*

A couple jurors told the family and police that what tipped the scales for them, in deciding first- or second-degree murder, was that Faelz had been stabbed forty-four times. If that number was smaller, they probably would have found Carlson guilty of second-degree murder. The quantity of the wounds made it first degree.

Drew Faelz didn't know how long the jury would take deliberating, so he wasn't in the courtroom when the verdict was announced. He was getting ready for a meeting at work, clutching his phone in his sweaty palm, when he received a text message. One of his co-workers had also attended Foothill High and knew the verdict could happen any minute. Drew pumped his fist, went out to his car to be alone, shed a few tears and couldn't wait to get home to be with his family.

"I never thought this would happen," Drew said. "I really didn't. It feels surreal. What does closure mean? I think I just really want to know why. I know he won't say anything. I want to ask him why. I want to know why. The closure is the doubt, as a kid, of being scared all the time that I could be next. Having the closure of closing this book. I don't have to worry about myself and my family. He's caught. We know who did it. And then it's justice for Tina."

What would his mother Shirley feel, if she were still alive?

"Just a relief," Drew said. "I remember where I was when she called me [after the arrest]. I was in my car. Just hearing the excitement in her voice. I think the trial would have been really tough on her at the same time. It would be a hard process to live through."

Steve Faelz wrote letters of appreciation to Pettigrew, the Pleasanton police chief, the district attorney and a few others. Even after the verdict, his emotions remained bittersweet. "The obvious reaction is the killer has been found," Steve Faelz said. "After thirty years, there's no doubt. That brings closure to that part of it. You always look back. What could I have done better? I'm sixty-six now. I certainly wasn't perfect as a father and wasn't perfect in my life. I've made a lot of mistakes. But you just wonder what could I have done to prevent this? I'm always going to have that as an issue to grapple with the rest of my life."

14
SENTENCING

I didn't do it, man!
—*Steve Carlson*

DECEMBER 30, 2014

Tanya Pittson still believes her brother is innocent. It's not because Steve told her this and she blindly believes him. Tanya doesn't believe he's innocent because she knows the real killer or because of evidence not presented at the trial or because she can provide his alibi.

It's just a gut feeling. She remembers that fateful night. Maybe not every detail, but she remembers a lot. She's considered getting hypnotized to see what memories might get rekindled. She swears the police were coming in and out of their house all afternoon and night, using their bathroom and drinking the coffee she made for them.

Tanya remembers multiple kids on the roof of their house, including Steve, watching the police work the crime scene. She never thought that her brother was exhibiting any unusual behavior, whatsoever, that night. And she recalls her mother coming home the next day, checking his room, checking all of his clothes and not finding anything suspicious.

Even after three years of frequent discussions about his defense, Tanya is not close to Steve. She hadn't spoken to him in almost twenty years before he was arrested. She admits that he's the quintessential example of what drugs, especially meth, will do to somebody.

When Steve complained that Tina Faelz's family was glaring at him during the trial, Tanya defended the victim's supporters. Tanya's response to her brother was:

> *They have actually handled themselves with such reverence. If you had lived your life differently, they wouldn't be trying to pin this on you. You made bad decision after bad decision. They believe you killed their daughter because the police told them that you did. They're not yelling obscene things at you. They lost their daughter. You have to have respect for them. They're not the ones bringing this against you. It's horrifying. But you have to take responsibility that you are here because you made bad, bad decisions.*

After the lecture, Tanya felt Steve got the message and stopped complaining about the family's glares.

You could make a compelling argument that Tanya has survivor's guilt. Her parents gave her love. They didn't give the same love to her siblings. They didn't know how to handle Steve. They cared more about having a good time themselves. On the day a girl was murdered across the street from their house, the parents were out of town partying and gambling, leaving the kids alone with no adult supervision. The parents didn't come home that night. They waited until the next day.

Tanya also comprehends that, at this point, she is all Steve's got. He is still family. She doesn't defend anything Steve did with all the various girls over the years. She was mortified when told Steve was briefly investigated concerning the disappearance of Ilene Misheloff, whose parents she knows personally, and deeply exhaled when told Steve couldn't be responsible because he had been in jail.

It's not easy visiting your brother in jail, listening to him ramble and barely able to understand him. It's not easy when he calls collect, rambles more and hands the phone to another inmate.

Steve Carlson wasn't expecting any family member to help his defense the way Tanya did. Carlson has the name of his friend Bonnie tattooed above his left eye. He wanted to get "Tanya" tattooed above his right eye out of respect for what she's done. Tanya declined the offer.

"I don't need that kind of tribute," Tanya said, with a laugh.

What if Tanya was ever given information that implicated her brother or if he confessed the murder to her? She's pondered this question frequently. Tanya said she would tell the police.

January 9, 2015

The sentencing for Steve Carlson was a heated day in the Rene C. Davidson Courthouse. It started when defense lawyer Annie Beles asked Alameda County Superior Court judge C. Don Clay to throw out the jury's verdict and grant Carlson a new trial.

Beles argued the DNA evidence should not have been allowed in the trial, that prosecutor Stacie Pettigrew presented no foundation regarding knife slippage to explain Carlson's blood on the purse and that the prosecution engaged in misconduct by "diluting the standard of proof" for guilt.

At one point, Beles said, "Does it matter what I say anymore? No. I'm ashamed. I fought for Mr. Carlson. I fought for the law to be presented to the jury in the correct way…I am ashamed to be a member of Alameda County and have this prosecutor do this and have it be allowed. Submitted."

"The record speaks for itself," Judge Clay said. "Based upon the evidence, the papers, the law, motion for new trial is denied."

Next came statements from the victim's family. Ron Penix traveled down from the state of Washington to speak about the biological daughter that he essentially gave up at an early age.

Tina Faelz with her mother, Shirley, and biological father, Ron Penix. *Courtesy of Karin Reiff.*

Penix didn't hold back his fury at Carlson, saying, "What's not fair is that this little girl never reached her full potential, and you've been able to breathe for the last thirty years. My hope for you is that for every second of every minute of every hour of every day for the rest of your pathetic life—"

Carlson interrupted, exclaiming, "I didn't do it, man!"

Penix continued, "—You will know the pain that Tina felt the last thirty seconds of hers. You are a piece of shit and God help you."

Beles objected to Penix's fiery words, calling them "an insult." Beles admitted her client has a drug problem, led a troubled life and committed crimes. But she said he's not a killer. "Fundamentally," Beles said, "he was a screw-up more than he was an evil man."

Judge Clay sentenced Carlson to twenty-six years to life in prison. No special circumstances existed to make Carlson eligible for the death penalty. Carlson is appealing the ruling.

TODD SMITH HAPPENED TO grow up a few houses away from where the Carlson family moved in 1980. By proximity and age, he and Steve became friends. They were never best friends. They delighted in smashing into each other at football practice. But they were friendly enough that Smith left campus to check on Carlson after he was locked in a dumpster one day at school. They were friendly enough that Smith initially lied to police about Carlson's whereabouts, wanting to protect him from a horrid crime that he didn't think any teenager was capable of committing.

A fateful conversation caused Smith to have strong suspicions about his friend. The next three decades were filled with gory images of Faelz's sliced-up body, follow-up questions from police, health issues, testimony on the witness stand the judge called "problematic" and endless haunting nightmares.

"I don't sleep," Smith explained. "I have vicious nightmares every night. My wife says I'm yelling in my sleep, cussing. I'm trying to kill people. They're trying to kill me. I'm fighting off people. This goes on every night...I wouldn't wish this on my worst enemy."

Smith attended the sentencing with his wife. Everything about the case was so sad, Smith said, he cried for ninety minutes straight. Smith slept for six hours, uninterrupted, the night of the conviction and the night of the sentencing. Those were the only two nights he could remember sleeping without getting up over the last three decades. He thought his nightmares—vivid, colorful, violent nightmares—were finally over for good. He was wrong.

"I still think about all the days that I've had horrible dreams and went to work with so little sleep," Smith said. "Yeah, he's in jail. It doesn't change how many lives were impacted by this. Katie Kelly, that poor girl, has been through heck and back too. She was smart enough to get counseling. I don't know why my parents didn't for me. Maybe my parents did, and I was so tough I didn't need it. I don't know. I can't blame my parents. I wish I'd have gotten counseling. I thought about it recently. It's probably not a bad idea."

Smith can't help replay that fateful day from 1984 in his brain.

"I wish I'd have listened to my mom when she said don't take my moped to school," he said. "I would have never been there to turn over Tina's body. It changed the whole course of the day—the timing of everything. I got home quicker. I got to pick up my brother quicker on our tandem bike. But I can't go back in time now."

JANET HAMILTON, THE MOTHER OF Carlson's ex-wife Justine, followed the trial from newspaper stories and this book's author. She considered attending the trial but elected to stay away. After everything she endured with Carlson in the 1980s and 1990s, she had no interest in seeing him again—even in a courtroom.

Hamilton reports that her granddaughter experienced some understandably tough years after her father's abandonment and mother's death. But she's doing well now and is surrounded by family and friends who love her.

Sarah Whitmire, the mother of Carlson's second child, is remarkably levelheaded considering her troubled teenage years and perilous pregnancy. She's been forced to live in shelters a few times, along with her child, but usually only for a month or two. She's very low income but manages to keep her apartment tidy, dresses her child in clean clothes and keeps their heads just barely above water.

Whitmire does not carry resentment toward Carlson. She realizes that Carlson will never fathom the pain and exhaustion he caused by forcing her to raise their child alone. When she lived in New York with her son, Whitmire would look out the window of a high-rise and beg the streets for a break, for some stranger to help her, because she often wondered if she was going to die.

She's now back in the general Sacramento area. Whenever giving up became an option, a random person would appear to help and make a difference. She used to write short stories and poems as a kid and remains a gifted writer.

"The world is an evil rough place, yet still speckled with flecks of humanity," Whitmire wrote. "Like the long flowers I would spot growing in the cracks of the never-ending pavement of New York City, kindness always finds a way to win. Without random acts of kindness, me and [my child] would never have survived."

On February 25, 2015, Carlson wrote to this author from San Quentin Prison. No changes were made to the grammar in his letter.

Josh

This is going to be a short letter. I am sorry I never sat down with you to give you my side of the story. I was legaly advised not to. Trust me I want to scream to the world my innocence!! I also want to thank you for treating my sister with kindness and respect. Thats why after this case gets overturned on appeal you are the only person Im going to talk to. I know you mean well by you writing this book. Josh I AM INNOCENT!! Anyways, Ill write you again once I get sent to the prison where Ill wait to hear from the appeal courts.

All my respect
Steven J. Carlson

BIBLIOGRAPHY

Bay Area Newspaper Group

Oakland (CA) Tribune

Pleasanton (CA) Patch

San Francisco Chronicle

Scott, Robert. *Rope Burns: Rape, Torture, and Murder...A Twisted Couple's Brutal Crime Spree*. Reissue ed. Bemidji, MN: Pinnacle Publishing, 2010.

ABOUT THE AUTHOR

Pleasanton native Joshua Suchon was a reporter at the *Oakland Tribune* for ten years before switching careers to pursue a lifelong dream to become a baseball play-by-play announcer. He's now the radio announcer for the Albuquerque Isotopes, the triple-A affiliate of the Colorado Rockies. This is his third book and first true crime. He can be reached at www.joshuasuchon.com.

Visit us at
www.historypress.net

This title is also available as an e-book